# (BE)WILDER

Darryl Jones is a Professor of Ecology at Griffith University in Brisbane, where for over 30 years he has been investigating the many ways that people and wildlife interact. He is particularly interested in why some species have been so successful in urban landscapes while many others have not, and how best to deal with the ensuing conflicts. His books include *Getting to Know the Birds in Your Neighbourhood*, *Feeding the Birds at Your Table* and *Curlews on Vulture Street* (all from NewSouth Publishing).

Dedicated to the memory
of Raymond Noel Jones
(31 Match 1936–9 June 2025)

And to all those who shared
these adventures with me.

# (BE)WILDER

## JOURNEYS in NATURE

Darryl Jones

NEWSOUTH

UNSW Press acknowledges the Bedegal people, the Traditional Owners of the unceded territory on which the Randwick and Kensington campuses of UNSW are situated, and recognises the continuing connection to Country and culture. We pay our respects to Bedegal Elders past and present.

**A NewSouth book**

*Published by*
NewSouth Publishing
University of New South Wales Press Ltd
University of New South Wales
Sydney NSW 2052
AUSTRALIA
https://unsw.press/

Our authorised representative in the EU for product safety is Mare Nostrum Group B.V., Mauritskade 21D, 1091 GC Amsterdam, The Netherlands (gpsr@mare-nostrum.co.uk).

© Darryl Jones 2025
First published 2025

10 9 8 7 6 5 4 3 2 1

A catalogue record for this book is available from the National Library of Australia

ISBN    9781761170386 (paperback)
        9781761179273 (ebook)
        9781761178443 (ePDF)

*Cover design* Madeleine Kane
*Cover illustrations* rawpixel, except Clouded leopard, Alamy
*Internal design* Josephine Pajor-Markus
*Printer* Griffin Press

UNSW
SYDNEY

# CONTENTS

# PREFACE

A WHEATEAR! THERE! ON THE TOP OF THAT RUSTY metal post, its white arse (the literal translation of its Old English name) obvious as it flew in. A slim, elegant bird, upright and alert. Its lovely tan-orange breast and slick bandit's mask give it a smart, no-nonsense look. I watch it watching me for a few minutes before it flits out of sight. About 50 metres further along, I spot another. And then a pair, directly ahead, hopping purposefully on the ground. None have taken the slightest notice of me.

Northern wheatears – to give them their full name – are in serious decline globally, but here they are unexpectedly abundant. I've seen them elsewhere in Europe but never more than one at a time. They are hardy birds, renowned for hanging out in tough, windswept places like high mountain meadows and Artic tundra. Places you might call picturesque, scenic, natural and remote.

Nothing like that here. In fact, the Flugplatz Johannisthal (Johannisthal Airfield) on the outskirts of Berlin could hardly be less 'natural'. It's a flat, neglected, degraded, weed-infested expanse, dotted with derelict buildings, and with slabs of broken concrete protruding from the rank grass at odd angles. Every surface has been excessively graffitied. It's an *ödland* (wasteland) or *freiraum* (empty space), as they say here. Or even *Rande der Hölle* (the outskirts of Hell), as our sceptical taxi driver described it. 'Why this place?' he said, when he dropped us off. 'There's nothing to see here.' He drove off shaking his head.

Why *have* I and a small group of colleagues come to this desolate place? It's a good question. The simplest answer is 'birds'. The wheatears, and a handful of other notable species as well: Eurasian skylarks, Eurasian kestrels, and red-backed shrikes, if we're very lucky. And some of the group are looking for butterflies and the shrubs they lay their eggs on. This seemingly desolate, weedy place is home to a remarkable variety of insects and plants. We are urban ecologists, interested in how some species can move successfully into places dominated by human activities and structures. When you think of somewhere wildlife could live within a city, it is likely to be gardens, parks or special conservation reserves. Places that provide shelter, foraging and breeding locations, and that usually look nice. But a surprising number of species have been able to colonise places that do not look nice.

'Friends, may I remind you to watch out for discarded concrete and fencing wire,' our local guide, Reiner, announces. 'This is a neglected industrial site with many trip hazards. So tread carefully.'

It's an important point. Unlike the usual places in cities that wildlife now happily occupy, this one is not people-friendly. You have to be willing to put up with a few risks to see northern wheatears here.

When ecologist Peter Meffert set out to investigate Berlin's wayward wheatears, he did not expect to find that their most successful breeding population – in the entire world – would be in a ruined industrial site. Yet there is a healthy male perched on a discarded sign (*Gefahr fernhalten*, 'Danger, Keep Away'), singing lustily in the late summer light, oblivious to the aesthetic values of humans. A short distance away, a neighbouring male returns the call. How could this delightful bird not just survive but positively thrive in such a disturbed and degraded place?

Among many discoveries, Peter found that these wasteland wheatears love to breed amid abandoned car parks or the concrete foundations of demolished buildings. When he published his findings, Peter wrote (his formal language not quite masking a level of incredulity) that despite the 'structural poorness of their breeding sites', more offspring were produced in these territories than in any other population throughout their entire range. He concluded that flat, open areas of asphalt and concrete were ideal if you wanted a clear view in all directions rather than beautiful surroundings. Aesthetics didn't appear to be a factor.

He also found that wheatears were remarkably tolerant of humans. Normally, they are difficult to approach; alert and flighty, they disappear long before you can get anywhere near them. Here, they barely seemed to notice us.

There is, indeed, little that is 'natural' about Johannisthal. Such areas are classified as 'brownspace': somewhere previously built upon, now vacant, awaiting future development or, as often as not, abandonment. Once a busy airfield, it's no longer a human-friendly space. That's one of the reasons it has been labelled 'unnatural'.

But a place doesn't have to be a toxic wasteland to be regarded as unnatural. Historically, anywhere occupied or even influenced by humans has been thought of by some as tainted and spoiled. Nature, it was declared, was something other-than-human, untouched by people. 'Natural', it followed, meant different, separate, distinct from humans. Such notions persist. If you seek nature, it is still implied – explicitly and implicitly – you need to find places without people. A distant national park, deep underwater, the top of a mountain.

If the more 'human' a place is, the less natural it is, then the very epitome of 'unnatural' must be a city. All over the world, people are moving from rural areas into big cities in ever-increasing numbers. Urban development is exploding, subsuming the surrounding lands as suburbs sprawl ever outwards. The scale and rapidity of urbanisation has made it one of the leading causes of extinction at the global scale in the current century. Now (since about 2007), for the first time in human history, more people live in cities than anywhere else. And whether it's a hundred-storey apartment tower or a gigantic estate of identical bungalows without backyards, the feeling that people are becoming increasingly isolated from nature is impossible to deny.

This progressive distancing from nature can have insidious effects, affecting our perception of anything non-human. Children who have never had the chance to interact with natural things – collecting leaves, watching tadpoles in a creek, building a shelter out of branches – can lose their curiosity about the natural world, a process known as the 'extinction of experience'. Unless you care about something, you don't want to learn more about it. This disconnection – 'ecological amnesia' – can lead to indifference and even hostility toward nature, reduced to a plastic plant or a television documentary; just another commodity.

This is alarming because it is now clear that a connection with nature is not just a pleasant background feature to our otherwise busy lives – something nice if you have the time, but not really a key part of who we are. Such an idea could not be more wrong or more dangerous. An exciting new field of research involving psychologists, neurologists, physicians and ecologists is discovering that being outside and connected to nature is critically important to our mental and physical wellbeing. And that includes everyone!

The evidence is overwhelming. Humans need regular exposure to nature, in whatever form it is available. It doesn't have to involve vigorous hiking in a distant national park; even small amounts of time in any green space can be beneficial. This could be simply spending time in your backyard, walking in the local park, or sitting on your balcony, listening to the birds; all such activities bring benefits. All contribute to feeling healthy and mentally balanced. And, remarkably, connection to nature is just like medicine: the benefits (measured in familiar ways such as stress hormone levels, blood pressure, time required for healing, etc.) accrue with dose rate. The more, the better – with no risk of overdosing.

Any form of connection with nature is good, but some aspects of this interaction appear to be better than others. The more intimate the connection, the greater the effect. This means that a casual walk in the park is fine, but being actively engaged in something while doing it is even better. Something like birdwatching, for example.

Which brings us back to this dilapidated industrial site in Berlin. No, it doesn't look 'natural' at all, but nature is here, and in a particularly impressive way. The discovery of a booming population of northern wheatears in a horrible, devastated landscape where nature appears to have been obliterated is a dramatic example of ecological resilience and recovery. If a seemingly fragile songbird can make such a place its home, what more is possible? What else have we missed? If nature can overcome the worst forms of destruction in a place of complete neglect, what might happen when we actively encourage biodiversity?

These are the questions that brought me here in the first place. Well, that and hoping to see the wheatears. You could say that it's just birdwatching. But making the effort to visit Flugplatz Johannisthal means more than the chance of adding another species to your life-list (or 'derelict airfield' list; birders have a lot of lists!). This desolate place is drawing birdwatchers from around the world who want to see an unlikely example of nature triumphing over adversity.

Birdwatching is a relaxing pastime in itself as well as an effective way of connecting with nature. For some people, it is a form of therapy, a way to reduce anxiety or build mental stability and resilience. It may also allow the possibility of hope at a time of almost universal environmental despair.

This book is an exploration of some of the many ways that people interact with nature. I could say 'connect with nature', but that sounds a bit too formal for something like birdwatching. Or experiencing a whale cruise. Or collecting wildflowers. All of these activities share something essential: a close interaction with the natural world.

I've provocatively started with a bunch of birdwatchers visiting a disused airfield in Europe. My point is that connecting with nature doesn't have to be done somewhere remote – in the Canadian Artic or the jungles of Borneo (though we will be going to both). I want to begin by challenging our notions of 'nature' and 'natural'. We could start by looking at definitions of these words, their changing meanings, their use in debates and arguments. But instead, let's see what British naturalist and writer Mark Cocker has to say about nature.

> Are you concerned about nature? And about how humans have done so much damage to the natural world? Do you imagine for a moment that we – you and I – are somehow separate from nature? If so, then ask yourself: what part of the food you ate for breakfast this morning, the book you are reading, the clothes you are wearing, the fuel which powers your car and your home, the air you breathe and the microbiome that occupies your own body and without which you could not even digest food? Which part of all of this is not of nature? Is not

natural? We are undeniably, inescapably, inextricably from and of the natural world. And it is high time we started to act as if we understood it to be so!

This is a book of stories about humans – including me – engaging with nature. Usually this involved interacting with wildlife of some sort (not always birds), but also places; sometimes both. It is a book that recognises that we are part of nature, and what that means. We have been subjected to the same evolutionary processes as all other species. But because of our outsized brains, we have come to wield enormous power. This has often been catastrophic for the rest of nature. It's time to act responsibility.

I have been thinking about and observing how people and wildlife interact for most of my life. I've been going out of my way to see wild animals all over the world, both the familiar and the very rarely seen. This has included some dramatic and dangerous encounters, as well as genuinely moving moments I can still hardly believe. Each one of these events revealed something about our (human) nature and 'nature' itself; how we can engage with wild animals in the ways that benefit us and don't impact the creatures.

I have tried to learn something from each of these events. Sometimes I have. Sometimes I still don't understand what happened. But every time, I have been changed in some way.

# INTRODUCTION

BEWILDERED.

Or perhaps chastened. Humbled, certainly. I'm sure there's a German word for being 'rendered speechless when confronted by one's ignorance'. But given the mix of being thoroughly perplexed and confused, 'bewildered' is pretty accurate. It happened a long time ago, but I recall my emotional state vividly.

This was my reaction to experiencing rainforest for the first time. It may sound a little melodramatic but, you see, I thought I knew all about rainforest. The impact of realising how little I understood was unexpectedly intense.

We were in a national park in Queensland, up in the mountains behind the Gold Coast. This was my first trip over the border of New South Wales since starting university in Armidale, a small rural town a few hours south of the border. It was the furthest north I had been in my whole life. Everything seemed somehow more exotic. The colours were brighter, the trees shaped differently; even the grass was, well, greener.

I had been thinking about rainforest for years. It seemed to be the epitome of nature at its most complex, an impossibly intricate system of connections between endless forms of life, each joined and interacting; a grand network, intertwined and interconnected. Networks within networks. At least, that was my superficial take from the textbooks, lectures and television documentaries I had devoured. It was effectively the opposite of the tame, truncated, open rural landscape I had grown up in. Rainforests represented nature, wild, prolific and exuberant; a place where an enthusiastic but naïve student could finally feel that they knew something about ecology.

The problem was, I had never seen actual rainforest. My impressions were entirely theoretical. Now I was about to see the real thing.

We arrived at the carpark of Springbrook National Park. My friends joined the crowd heading towards the lookout. I went in the opposite direction, where a path led towards a dense wall of forest. I followed. And within a few steps, the bright Queensland sunshine disappeared; I was instantly in a completely different universe, unlike anything I had experienced before.

It was dark, moist and unsettling. In every direction, plants proliferated in a silent explosion of abundance: an impossibly complicated labyrinth of intertwined vines, thickets of spiny tendrils, hundreds of thin saplings. Trees of every dimension shot arrow-straight towards the unseen sky. My gaze followed a broad mossy trunk slowly upward. The interlocked foliage far above formed a solid layer, blocking out the light, apart from a few thin shafts illuminating small patches of the forest floor. A thick carpet of dead leaves, moss-covered branches and fungi covered every part of the ground. It was quiet and still, all outside noise thickly dampened. A rich, dank, earthy smell of decomposition and damp soil permeated everything.

It was too much. There were too many different types of living things. Too many trees and vines and shrubs jammed together. It was too complicated and wild. Too different. Too alien. In every direction, on every surface, strange living things grew vigorously, reaching out, grabbing, choking. There were plants on plants on plants. Weird hair-like blue-grey 'beards' of fibres hung from swooping lianas and looping vines. I sensed a myriad of tiny beings watching, breathing, consuming, moving, oblivious to the gaping human a few metres away.

City-based Malaysian writer Tan Twan Eng had a similar reaction:

> It's hard to describe what entering a rainforest is like.
> Conditioned to the recognisable lines and shapes
> one sees every day in towns and villages, the eyes are
> overwhelmed by the limitless varieties of saplings,
> shrubs, trees, ferns and grass, all exploding into life
> without any apparent sense of order or constraint.

I backed out, into the sunshine, unnerved and shocked by my reaction. I didn't understand – or couldn't, not then.

Eventually, my response to rainforest became one of profound awe and respect. Within a few years, I would be spending much of my time immersed in this extraordinary ecosystem, acutely aware of how little I actually knew or understood. But on that first encounter, the confrontation between my supposed knowledge and the uncontrolled reality was not simply confusing, it was almost belittling. Mortifying.

That experience – something I have never tried to articulate or discuss with anyone – had a long-lasting impact. How could I have been so arrogant, so simplistic, so hubristic? It instilled in me the beginnings of a more realistic, possibly more humble way of thinking about the natural world. Not instantaneously, of course; I was 18 and male, after all! But it was a fundamental first step.

IT'S FOUR DECADES LATER AND I AM FEELING thoroughly bewildered once again, though for different reasons. I'm driving up the steep, convoluted road towards the well-known rainforest resort of Binna Burra. The name comes from the Yugambeh–Bundjalung language group, and means 'place of beech trees'. This famous place is in Lamington National Park, a sprawling reserve that hugs the precipitous cliff edge along the Queensland–New South Wales border. It's not far from Springbrook, although a broad valley separates the two mountain ranges on which they are situated. The narrow road initially traversed lush cattle pastures and eucalypt forest before zigzagging through subtropical rainforest as it reached the top of the plateau.

It's been a sobering drive.

I pull up in the Binna Burra carpark and look around. I am stunned. There's nothing left. Instead of the collection of rustic wooden buildings set among the rainforest, all that remains are blackened concrete slabs and twisted sheets of corrugated iron roofing. Most of the buildings which used to spread in an arc around the iconic lodge were obliterated by a fire on 10 September 2019. The loss of Binna Burra shocked the nation. The initial reaction was one of disbelief. How could this have happened? It was in a rainforest!

For some time after the fires, I had been reluctant to see what had happened for myself, anticipating anguish and shock at what I might find. Now, almost four years later, my emotions are a mixture of regret and relief; the signs of destruction are all too evident, yet so are signs of resilience and recovery. Scanning the landscape that plunges away to the north, evidence of the fires is still starkly clear. Blackened trunks punctuate a wide apocalyptic landscape, indicating something of the scale of the devastation.

Not everywhere has been burnt. Some of the steep gullies escaped the inferno and maintain the typical grey-green tinge of gum trees. Where the flames had scoured the forest, however, the colour scheme was from a radically revised palette: shockingly green new leaves against a backdrop of charred black trunks. Life has returned as a boisterous explosion of fresh foliage, vivid and exuberant, showing where the forest was composed of eucalypts.

Higher up, however, where flames had stormed into the rainforest, the colours are very different. The few trees that had not been completely incinerated still stand, now black and dead. Instead of the usual open, dimly lit underworld beneath a continuous canopy, vast areas have been brutally exposed, the light enabling an explosion of shrubs and thicket species, mostly invasives such as lantana. These blanket the burnt areas in mottled brown and dark greens.

Lamington National Park, declared in 1915, exists primarily because of the expanse of subtropical rainforest, an ecological novelty in a vast continent dominated by eucalypts. This large park is a rare mix of subtropical and, at higher altitudes, temperate plant communities dominated by Antarctic beech. The lower slopes are all eucalyptus and casuarina, wattle and banksia, all fire-adapted plants. All of these trees and shrubs need fire to reproduce, though some are more tolerant than others. The heat and sometimes simply the smoke is necessary to induce the germination of their seeds.

At a certain point, where the basaltic soils start, the nature of the forest changes abruptly. Suddenly, it's rainforest. Wet, humid, dark, dank. Therefore, logically, inflammable. Rainforests don't burn, not because they can't but simply because they are usually too damp. Generally, bushfires in Australia occur where and when it's hot and dry, which is mainly in the hotter months in the south of the continent. In the north at that time of the year, it's hot but also wet and humid.

Queenslanders have traditionally been grateful, if not smug, in the certain knowledge that catastrophic bushfires don't happen in their state as they do in southern parts. Bushfires obviously still occur in Queensland, and sometimes they are serious. But not in summer, and not in rainforest. Never in rainforest.

The news that wildfires were raging though subtropical rainforest was yet another unbidden, unwelcome lesson in severe reality – and humility. It forced a reluctant rethink of what was normal, or even plausible.

The loss of the historic Binna Burra Lodge received widespread media coverage, throughout Australia and internationally. It was a big story. But not for long.

The Lamington fires were simply the first alarming flashpoints in what was to become the worst environmental catastrophe in Australia's modern history. The severity, scale and intensity of the Black Summer fires of 2019–20 changed enormous areas of the continent forever. Some places will take centuries to recover. Some never will.

IN LATE NOVEMBER 2021, ALMOST TWO FULL YEARS after the Black Summer fires, I drove along the Snowy Mountains Highway from Tumut through Kosciuszko National Park to the Victorian border. Near the famous Yarrangobilly Caves, the iconic snow gum forest, once a broad sweep of dark emerald foliage, had been replaced by a million jagged white skeletons. From horizon to horizon. This time there was no epicormic growth – which is when shoots grow from dormant buds under the tree's bark – that vibrant, reassuring sign of life continuing that defines resilience in most eucalypts, and shows that life can rise from the ashes. Indeed, most eucalypts rely on periodic fires for the germination of their seeds, which wait down in the leaf litter. As adult trees, most species bounce back even from a serious grilling, the blackened trucks festooned with bright green leaves within weeks.

Not snow gums. They can't shrug off intense fire. It's not something they have experienced much, if at all, during their long evolutionary history, growing slowly on frigid mountaintops. They could probably withstand a low intensity blaze, such as practised by the Wiradjuri, Wolgalu, Ngunnawal and Monaro Ngarigo who lived throughout the region. But Black Summer in the Snowy Mountains incinerated everything, utterly, including the organic matter far below the surface. Not even the soil bacteria and specialised root fungi essential for most plant life survived. Given enough time, these areas will eventually be again covered in vegetation. But it won't be a snow gum forest.

I TRAVELLED TO BINNA BURRA PARTLY TO CONFRONT my fears. As I forced myself to look at the violently altered landscape spread out below, the space where the grand old lodge used to be and the bright green sheen of the rapidly growing understorey, it seemed like an appropriate place to reflect, demonstrating as it did both the scale of the changes being wrought on nature, as well as its resilience. An opportunity to grapple with the reality of human impacts and our collective reluctance to do anything about it. To face the frightening reality of living in the Anthropocene.

The fires were followed by floods – shocking but well predicted symptoms of the climate crisis. Fire and flood are brutal but inescapable components of this continent. They have become colourful though violent parts of our folklore. This makes it possible to think that these elemental forces are normal features of the continent, natural phenomena, allowing statements such as 'The climate is always changing' to be commonly heard. Tragic, but we'll get over it. Carry on as before. Things will get back to normal. No big deal.

Except that it is a very big deal! Those fires and floods were next level 'unprecedented'. They have literally *never happened before*. Bushfires in rainforest. Several 'one-in-five hundred years' floods in a decade. Out-of-control fires in more than two hundred locations on the same day. Over three billion animals burnt to death.

This is not normal or natural. Something has changed, and it's bad.

Unfortunately, the list of shocking 'natural' phenomena just keeps growing. Massively destructive cyclones, prolonged droughts, blistering heat for weeks on end, vast areas of coral reef bleaching. All natural, yes, but exacerbated enormously by the warming climate. And all predicted with awful certainty by climate scientists. All of these catastrophes are going to become 'normal' occurrences in the near future, if they haven't already.

And when you add the extinction crisis, escalating habitat destruction, universal microplastics and lethal air pollution – to name just a few attendant terrors – it is no mystery that climate grief is a genuine syndrome, and growing fast. With horrifying images of environmental catastrophe inescapable – all media including the socials abound in confronting visuals – it doesn't take much to push people over the edge. Despondency and despair seem like reasonable responses in the circumstances.

But that's not going to do any good. We've been there many times before. Despite instinctively wanting to curl up in a ball and give up, we simply can't. It might already be too late, but heading down the dead end of hopelessness is simply not an option.

The stories presented in this book attempt to engage and stimulate, enrage and inspire, activate and illuminate. We desperately need stories right now, because they make us challenge certainty. Being utterly convinced about something can lead to conformity, bigotry, ignorance and intolerance. The advent of the Anthropocene has forced us to confront our biases and pointless pettiness. We no longer have the luxury of arguing about light bulbs or plastic straws. We need to take this seriously. Right now!

To be bewildered is to be overwhelmed, confused and rendered ineffectual. To feel powerless in the face of seemingly impossible difficulties. This had been the perspective of those who were thrust – or sometimes chose to travel – into the wilderness. The exiles, prophets, lunatics and adventurers. For them, the wilderness was, by definition, empty, lonely and difficult. A place of danger and extreme risk.

Yet wilderness was also a place of insight and wisdom, though this was hard-earned, requiring immense inner strength and even greater mental discipline. Many prophets and mystics – and Jesus himself – sought refuge from the human world. After severe physical and psychological testing, they returned, renewed and refreshed. Wilderness as a source of hope and inspiration.

I would like to suggest that we take this optimistic understanding of the wild and use it as positive and active motivation. Rather than being 'bewildered' by the catastrophes we see all around us, we should 'be wilder' in our actions and engagement. It's possibly our only hope.

Be wilder.

# (1)
## WHEN BIRDS BECAME COOL

NED McGOWAN IS NO ENVIRONMENTALIST. 'LOOK, I'm no farken greenie!' he says for the third time, just to be sure. And loud enough that everyone in this noisy beer garden hears him clearly.

He slams his VB down on the wooden tabletop and glares around at the blokes at the next table, daring anyone to say a word. Eyes averted, the conversations resume, perhaps a little quieter than previously. I'm beginning to wonder why I'm here, whether this was a mistake.

Ned leans ominously toward me, fixes me in a fierce stare and then says something I would never have expected.

I was back in my hometown, Wagga Wagga, passing through on my way to a conference in Brisbane. The trip was going to be too brief to see anyone except my parents. Or so I thought. My father had run into his friend Ned at the local shopping centre a few days before. When Dad mentioned I was arriving shortly, Ned became uncharacteristically keen to meet me. 'I've got something to tell him. It might be important.' He wouldn't elaborate, so they had agreed that when I arrived, we should go straight to the local pub on the way from the airport. He would be waiting in the beer garden.

'He was pretty serious about wanting to see you,' Dad said by way of explanation as we pulled into the carpark beside the pub. Mum – who, in time-honoured tradition, had been looking forward to serving me a cup of strong tea, her signature rock-like Anzacs and telling me what was wrong with the Australian cricket team – was not impressed. 'Silly old fool. What could be this important?' she muttered from the backseat. ('More important than tea and cricket,' I added in my mind.)

I knew Ned more by reputation than acquaintance. He was one of those ex-farmers who had settled unhappily into town after a lifetime on the land. He and Winnie, his wife of almost sixty years, had the rest of their lives planned out in detail: cruises, plays, trips to the Sydney Opera House, and interstate visits to see the grandkids. Ned had been more-or-less happy to go along with whatever Winnie had in mind. But only a few months after moving into their tiny flat in the suburbs of Wagga, Winnie had succumbed to pancreatic cancer. It was all over in a few terrible weeks. For the first time in his life, Ned found himself alone and completely unprepared. Winnie had taken care of every aspect of their lives. He was bereft. He became morose and agitated. Dad was one of the few old friends who put up with him.

In what seemed like a spur-of-the-moment decision, Ned sold the flat and purchased a 'useless rocky hill' a short distance out of town. He moved into the large shed on the site and became something of a recluse. The only time he came into town was on Friday afternoons, when he purchased a few groceries before settled into the Blamey's beer garden. That's where we found him, impatiently awaiting our arrival.

We join Ned at the rough wooden table. After only a perfunctory handshake, he leans towards me, fixes me with an intense stare.

'Have you seen my Facebook today?' he says.

Taking my open-mouthed expression – correctly – as a 'no', Ned picks up his phone, muttering quietly ('Farken fat thumbs …') as he searches for something. 'Found it. Here. Look,' he says, showing me the screen, his face alight with a crooked grin. 'Not very clear, but you can make it out.'

The image is dark and out of focus, but there, on the leafy ground, is a small plump bird with long spindly legs and a fierce, defiant expression.

'Is that a –'

'White-browed scrubwren. Yep. Howsabout that!'

Ned looks back at the phone, beaming. 'Never thought I got them out at my place. It's pretty dry and rocky. But the callistemon hedges I planted a few years back seemed to have done the trick, gives the little birds somewhere to hide. Yeah, I got soldier birds. Noisy farken miners! There're everywhere. Not much we can do about that, except give some shelter for the little ones they always chase. And I've been dealing with the cats. You should come out and see for yourself. Bring the Old Man. We might get him interested yet!'

Ned McGowan is probably the least likely convert

to birdwatching I've yet to encounter. There was little to predict this transformation. He had been a traditional farmer, focused on wheat, canola and fat lambs. Some birds – ravens, birds of prey, bee-eaters – he regarded as harmful vermin that needed to be 'actively discouraged' (in other words, shot). A very small few were 'good', meaning useful. For example, the ibis that turned up when grasshoppers were plentiful. And owls, which consumed mice and rats. Most birds, however, were irrelevant to farm-related output and were therefore ignored. A farmer had plenty to worry about without needing to think about the merely 'pretty' or 'interesting'.

Yet, here he was, excited about scrubwrens!

Later, when we eventually get home and the long-delayed tea and Anzacs have been produced, it is Dad who surprises me with a plausible explanation.

'When Winnie died, Ned went downhill fast. He argued and complained, saw only the bad side of everything. Most of his old mates gave up on him, which only made things worse.

'When he bought the land, I thought he was running away. He probably was. I worried he might turn into a complete hermit.'

But something happened. He slowed down and started to notice things around him. Reptiles, butterflies and, of course, birds. There were always plenty around the spring-fed creek near the shed, the only reliable water on the place. It took a while, but he changed. The birds were busy getting on with their lives. Maybe he should do the same.

'Yes, birds!' he'd told Dad, in strict confidence (he

didn't want anyone to think he had gone soft). 'I hadn't taken any notice of them before. They just didn't figure in my life. But they can teach us, they can. They didn't mope and whinge. Life's too short to be negative. They taught me a lesson. Gave me a kick up the bum! "Pick yourself up, you stupid old bugger, and do something useful."'

'He's a lot happier,' Dad continues. 'Got stuck into planting hedges of native shrubs – a tough job in that dry, rocky country. I was relieved to see him recover so well, but now he never shuts up about his bloody birds!'

Dad is no psychologist and certainly not much of a philosopher, but he had a point. When people have the chance to stop and look around, sometimes they see things they were too busy and preoccupied to notice before. Like birds.


LIFE. IT NEVER STOPS.

Until it does.

Suddenly everything changed. A certain microscopic nonliving virus appeared out of nowhere and transformed the entire planet.

The whole world was forced to stop everything and pay attention. It was so massive and potentially catastrophic that cities, states and eventually entire countries stopped. Stopped moving, stopped planning, stopped doing what they had always done. Moving around became extremely constrained; in many places, even being outside the home was extremely limited. Apart from a select few professions (police, medical workers, security enforcers, house renovators(!)), people almost everywhere on the planet were locked down. The severity varied but most people experienced some degree of imposed restriction on their movements. This lasted from a few to many months. In some cases, people were seriously constrained for years.

Roads were deserted, trains stopped running, planes were grounded. When some movement was eventually allowed, it was limited to the immediate vicinity: the house-yard, surrounding streets or a nearby park. The standard mode of transport became walking. Seemingly overnight, the world reverted to pre-industrial modes of doing and being.

The world became local. The focus was on the nearby and close-up. When you walk rather than drive, you have time to think and observe. Everyone became explorers of their immediate patch. Remarkable and mundane discoveries were made daily.

And one of the biggest discoveries? Birds! They seemed to be everywhere. Had they always been there, but we were all too busy to notice? Certainly, in the absence of vehicles, planes and trains, the world was much quieter. Lives less hectic. Perhaps for the first time in their lives, people heard and appreciated birdsong. It was ubiquitous. And delightful. People realised that some birds had gorgeous voices. Other were loud and outrageous. Or just strange. They had been there the whole time, but no one had noticed.

And just like that, the world became obsessed with birds. It was a genuinely global phenomenon. Prescient researchers all over the world realised early on that something big was happening and began to record this unlikely revolution. A plethora of articles has since been published, showing that interest in birds rose everywhere during the first lockdown. People desperately wanted to know more, as indicated by astronomic levels of internet searches for a range of topics associated with birds. Sales of binoculars and field guides surged. Bird feeders and seed mixes sold out. Neighbours swapped sightings and argued about identifications. Bird blogs, chat sites and social media groups exploded. At least it was something to think about other than invisible deadly viruses.

The various reasons underlying this Covid-generated worldwide fascination with birds are still being discussed. There are a lot of potential influences, but one seems particularly pertinent: the birds were carrying on as though there was no pandemic. As the *New York Times* put it: 'The birds are not on lockdown'. They didn't seem to notice. They weren't cowering in fear or hoarding toilet paper. They were out and about, just like always, being beautiful, oblivious, independent. They seemed to be making a statement: *life continues, hope is possible.*

Ned McGowan wouldn't have used those words, but would have agreed, I'm sure. Though probably not out loud.

Others were more forthcoming. A young woman I met at a bookshop in Sydney was explicit: 'Birds saved me. Literally. I was living alone in the UK, far from friends and family, unable to travel home, or anywhere. I became seriously depressed. Then one day in my tiny garden, a robin appeared. I hadn't noticed it previously.

It sat on a wall a few metres away, looked me in the eye and sang so powerfully I stopped thinking about my troubles and listened. The bird seemed to be singing just for me, saying something like: "Look around you. There is life and beauty. Hope and purpose. Don't be so self-centred. Get out and start living!"'

For others, the birds were a reminder of childhood, favourite family activities and places they had visited. Everyone had their own reasons for enjoying birds.

Some people watch birds simply to occupy the time. For others, the beauty of even familiar species can inspire jaw-dropping awe. The first time someone focuses their binoculars on a rainbow lorikeet or even a starling can be a life-changing experience. Seeing the intricacy of the feathers and their vibrant colours can change one's appreciation of even commonplace birds in an instant. Being able to see them up close through your 'bins' (as binoculars are often called) can be a revelation.

What these people wanted was know who these birds were. To be able to give them a name. Identify them. You can't talk about them or ask questions if you can't name the specific bird you are talking about. But where do you start?

THE LIGHTS IN THE AUDITORIUM DARKEN. THE cacophony of voices subsides. The enormous screen comes to life, displaying a satellite image of Australia and the scattering of islands directly to the north. The contrast between the dry orangey red of most of Australia and the deep green of Papua New Guinea is stark. Chris Wood is on stage, speaking to a room full of researchers, students, professional ornithologists and hardcore bird fanatics from all around the world. We are in Brisbane for the bi-annual Australasian Ornithological Congress. Some of the biggest names in bird science and conservation have turned up to this session, eager to hear about the latest developments in eBird, the flagship program of the Cornell Lab of Ornithology. Everyone uses eBird. Chris is the program's manager. He told me that his title sounds too formal for the amount of fun he has.

I'm almost certain that none of us expects what happens next.

'Pretty smart audience here today,' Chris notes cheekily. 'More PhDs per row than your average crowd. Plenty of mega-twitchers with shockingly long life lists, I'd suspect. Academics with H-scores in the stratosphere. All in all, a pretty sharp audience, we'd all agree?'

There is nervous laughter in the crowd, the dimly lit room hiding our apprehensive expressions. Where exactly is he going with this?

'Set your egos to the side for a moment and watch the screen. I've picked a bird familiar to many of you – the eastern koel – to illustrate my point. This species is here in Brisbane right now. I'm sure some of you have heard their persistent, if not exasperating, calls of "ooo-OOOOO". There are plenty of records for this species on eBird. Let's see what happens when we roll progressively through all of the location records for a whole year.'

Each individual koel record is shown as a single blue

dot, but at the scale of a continent, there are so many that it looks like a steadily moving wave. From June to August – winter in the southern hemisphere – the huge island of Papua New Guinea is mottled blue almost everywhere; these are koels hanging out in the tropical rainforest during the non-breeding season. At that time of the year, there are none in Australia. The entire continent is blank.

As the animation moves into late August, a dramatic change occurs. A wave of blue suddenly forms and moves south and begins to trickle, then flood, into Australia. Starting at Cape York, the closest point to Papua New Guinea, the wave of blue flows steadily all the way down the east coast as far as Victoria. By the end of January, the transfer is complete: not a single koel remains in Papua New Guinea, while about half of Australia is now red, indicating that they were breeding when the record was made.

It's a spectacular presentation. And it isn't simply an artist's impression of the bird's movements. Although the colours are an artefact, what is displayed are actual locations where the birds were seen: 86 149 times ordinary birdwatchers made the observation and sent it to eBird.

'That's a decent tally for a bird notoriously difficult to see and that lives half the time in extremely remote locations. Of course, most of these records will have been identified by call only. But there's no mistaking this species.'

'You know what I find astonishing about this data?' Chris continues. 'It's that the so-called experts, the professional researchers and consultants and full-time birders, people like us, provided a trivial proportion of all this data. What is genuinely exciting is that almost all of it was submitted by ordinary birders dedicating their time to recording birds wherever they are and submitting them. People like this.'

The map vanishes and a video starts. It's a TikTok 'story', so we are told. Many of us would not know TikTok from Instagram. But the people on the screen certainly do! A rapidly changing gallery of young people appears. Moving to the beat of the soundtrack, they talk enthusiastically about bird identification. With staccato editing and pulsating music, kids as young as ten rave about the Merlin app, how to use it and what makes it so cool. These are kids! Rapping about bird ID! And giving advice on how to get your ID right! It is a stark example of how much the image of birding has changed.

'These people should be our target audience. Not copies of us, pale and stale. We need to be engaging everyone to enjoy their birds. And if we do it properly, they may start to embrace nature. It might be the most important thing we can do.'

THE CORNELL LAB OF ORNITHOLOGY HAS BEEN ONE of the most influential organisations in the world when it comes to encouraging people to engage in natural history projects. While some form of amateur involvement in science projects has been around since 1900, when the Audubon Society organised the first Christmas Bird Count, it was the Cornell Lab that formalised Citizen

Science as a sound and reliable means of collecting data on birds.

It didn't take much thought to realise that one of the richest sources of information about birds resided in the notebooks virtually every birder has kept, often from childhood. It's a given that birdwatchers list everything. The problem is that zillions of such notebooks sit forgotten in drawers or in dusty boxes in the attic. If only all of that information could be gathered together, organised in sensible ways and then made available to anyone who wanted to use it. What a resource that would be!

After lots of trials and discussion, a small team at the Lab came up with the idea of eBird. It started in a humble way back in 2002, as simply somewhere that birders could store their records in a central location. Today, 'humble' is no longer an appropriate description. In 2022, its twentieth anniversary year, a total of over 1.3 billion records had been received from more than 820 000 participants. The amount of information now available on species from all over the world is almost impossible to comprehend. A range of studies based on this data has been already undertaken. There is almost no end to the questions that can be asked. Undoubtedly, detailed investigations are going to transform many ideas we currently have about birds. Already, hundreds of studies utilising this information have been published (and listed on the eBird website under 'Science'), providing details on bird behaviour and movements – for example, the surprising movement of birds into the massive new cities in China, where parks are established before the people move in. On the other hand, the data is showing in sobering detail how the abundance of many species is changing, almost always downwards.

As the animations of the koel migrations revealed, the level of detail now available is extraordinary. And yes, fancy technology has enabled stunning visual presentations, while supercomputers search for patterns and anomalies. But it's important to remember that all of this is only possible because untrained, ordinary folks from literally every country in the world have been willing to sign up and send in their sightings. eBird is now by far the biggest citizen science project ever undertaken.

But you have to ask: why? Why are so many people enthusiastically participating in something that most are unlikely to use themselves? Although the eBird database is available, for free, to anyone with a legitimate reason to use it, it's mainly academics, researchers, professional ornithologists, environmental scientists and consultants who do so.

Not Dawn Muir, who just visited 'her' patch, a small wetland she visits every Thursday morning, early. 'If I'm lucky, I'll finish my rounds just before Book Club. If I'm late, it's because I've seen something unusual. I always tell the girls the highlights, even though they mock me. But Clare, our youngest member, asked last week whether she could come and see what it's all about. You never know what might happen!'

# (2)
## TIMING is EVERYTHING

*Day three in the Arctic and my first long walk. The hut is somewhere behind me but has disappeared behind the rise. I turn around slowly, taking it all in. Almost the entire landscape is covered in snow, a thousand different hues of white. It's not flat, but endless uneven undulations. I've never been in such a vast yet featureless place. The monotonous endlessness is unsettling; I feel exposed, vulnerable; there's nowhere to hide or shelter. I'm looking, but there's nothing to focus on.*

*Wait ... there's something. Way over there ... That! What is it? It's white – well, everything is. It seems to be quite far away ... not sure how far, though. Depends how big is it. I don't think it moved. Maybe just a strange boulder?*

TORONTO AIRPORT IS HUGE, CAVERNOUS AND SO noisy it's almost impossible to concentrate. Like everyone else, I'm staring up at the gigantic Arrivals and Departures screen. It's constantly changing: flickers, scrolls, stops, scrolls again. It's happening so fast, no one can find what they're looking for. A murmuring, dysfunctional aggregation of anxious people is assembled beneath, every face straining towards the ever-changing screen, urgently scanning for the fragments of information that matter to them.

The main focus is on the column to the far right. Every time the screen reconfigures, new CANCELLED or DELAYED labels appear in alarming red. Every time the scrolling stops, there is a momentary pause from the crowd before gasps and expletives erupt. Gesticulations. Middle fingers. Wild-eyed casting around for someone to blame or shout at. Storming off to rage at airline staff. There's a growing sense of apprehension, possibly inevitable doom. Those unaffected are tense, wondering if or when their flight will be cut. Trying not to think about consequences: tight schedules, missed connections, dashed hopes, altered plans.

A man in his forties turns to me, a complete stranger, and says with a mixture of exasperation, anger and fear, 'My mother-in-law's gunna kill me!', before pushing his way through the crowd.

Outside, far away to the north-west, a massive Arctic storm cell is sweeping towards us, smothering vast swathes of North America in deep swirling snow, burying cars and roads, inconveniencing millions, and bringing almost all travel to a jarring halt.

So far, the blizzard has buried a wide band west of Lake Superior. Our intended destination in the north-eastern part of Canada is far above the danger zone. But Toronto, where we are nervously waiting, is directly in the path of the approaching storm. Our schedule is tight and inflexible. A single cancelled flight threatens the entire trip. Miss just one of our four connections and the whole project – months in preparation – is in jeopardy. Everything will need to be rethought from scratch. Or abandoned altogether.

*Ding, ding, ding,* in ascending tones: the public address system again has something to say. Everyone hushes to listen. Instead of the dreaded *We regret to inform …,* it's something different, normal: 'Canadian North flight ST101 to Ottawa will be departing from Gate 54. Please make your way to the departure lounge immediately.'

I might get to see the Arctic after all.

I THOUGHT ESTIMATING SIZE USING SPATIAL PER-spective was universal, or at least natural. That wherever you were, you could work out the general size of something, mentally compensating for the fact that things get smaller with distance. But I'm starting to realise there is more to it than I expected. Working out the size of distant objects is more than simply looking. There needs to be something for comparison, a familiar object like a car, a house, an electricity pole – things that provide some sort of scale. But not too big or far away; mountains aren't much help.

Most of the time we don't need to think about these computations; our minds do it for us. We only need to take note or be alert if there's a good reason, or perhaps a risk. If I had actually thought about perspective before, it would only have been as a concept. Something theoretical, not concrete, not real. Certainly not a life-and-death situation. Relatively speaking.

This place has no cars or mountains or telephone poles. All I've got for comparison are our tents and the mess hut, and both are currently out of view. The entire snow-covered landscape recedes towards the horizon without any useful reference points for size. The general visual impression is that it's spectacularly unremarkable. The gently undulating terrain is confoundingly featureless.

It's different at ground level. Dotted around are a few patches where the snow has melted. Surrounding my boots is a mosaic of dull green-grey mosses, lichens and grasses; even a few subdued flowers. There are even 'trees': Arctic willows, miniature and prostrate, bonsaied into the horizontal by the brutal, unrelenting Arctic winds. Raise your eyes and those subtle details disappear. The off-white landscape spreads unevenly away in every direction, offering no certainty about how far away – or how big – anything might be.

I've been taking in this view for an hour or so, feeling increasingly but pleasantly disorientated. This is unlike any landscape I have ever been in, and I'm determined to make the most of the experience.

*Oh! The white thing way over there just moved. Shit! Yes, it's definitely slowly moving to the right. So it's not a boulder. And I have absolutely no idea how big it is, or how far away. Or even what it is.*

THERE ARE SIX OF US. EVERYONE ELSE IS FROM Queens University in Ontario, almost 7000 kilometres directly south. I am the only non-Canadian, still not quite believing I have made it to the Arctic. Getting here from Toronto required multiple stages, involving four different planes, each smaller than the last. The final one was a draughty, cramped and extremely noisy Twin Otter, the aerial Land Rover of the Far North.

The last leg of the journey was the most sobering. In the hamlet of Sanirajak, on the extreme north-east coast of Canada, I had wandered the short streets, watched Inuit kids kicking a dirty soccer ball in the powdery grey dirt, bought a Coke and a Hershey bar from the only shop and wondered whether I had ever been anywhere so remote. I hadn't, but Sanirajak was New York City compared to our final destination.

The plane bounced down the makeshift runaway and crawled laboriously into the air, shuddering and tilting from side to side. The land below looked like a different planet. A monotonous carpet of colourless dull white in all directions. There were no roads, no houses, no human or even notable natural features anywhere. A shudder of anxiety mixed with excitement shot through me.

Sarcpa Lake, latitude 68° North, is (just) above the Arctic Circle (which, technically, is the band around the top of the planet at exactly latitude 66° 33", in case you were wondering). Within this zone, mid-summer has continual daylight, and winter the opposite: long, long bitter months of total, frozen darkness.

The plane skidded to a dusty halt beside a solitary grey hut. The screaming, grating engine noise ceased abruptly and we stepped out into an almost vacuum-like silence. The auditory change was dramatic; I wondered whether I had suddenly lost my hearing. No, it's just that there was almost no ambient sound – only our voices, the crunch of boots on gravel, the sharp knock of metal crates being stacked. A distant liquid bird call seemed unnaturally clear in the still air. Our normal voices were way too loud.

A ranger who had been waiting beside his skidoo waited until we had assembled, walked over. He looked uncertain and gave a weak smile.

'Welcome. My name is Luke Avaalaaqiag. Full name is too hard so I'm usually just Luke A. You are in Nunavut country. I know you want to start exploring, but I'm obliged to run through some health and safety procedures.'

Professional obligations, bureaucracy, legal requirements – yes, obviously these things are all important, especially out here. But my mind was not on Luke's speech.

I gazed around, taking in the strangeness of the monotonous expanse surrounding us, suddenly aware of the clear, frigid air. It smelled of incongruous elements: stale water, diesel, manure, humus … and the air was ice cold, painfully so. Intuitively, I didn't dare breathe deeply; that could be dangerous to delicate lungs. A pale, almost white sun, which seemed much further away than normal, floated low in the sky, devoid of warmth. Its light was so insubstantial we didn't even cast shadows.

Luke was still talking.

'Finally, something important: we do get polar bears

out here. Used to be very rare, but are more common these days', he said with a little more emphasis, the standard finale to his too-often repeated speech. The others didn't seem to notice, but it got my attention.

'This means you must be careful. Keep your eyes open and always carry one of these flare guns.' He held up a bright red plastic pistol that looked like a cheap kid's toy with an abnormally large barrel.

'These only shoot flares, not bullets. Fire only if you are certain the bear has seen you and is approaching. Do. Not. Shoot. It. At the bear. That would only make them angry. Fire it high in the air so others can find you. Only in a real emergency, obviously. But if the bear is coming toward you and you are far from camp or other people, there is not much you can do.'

WE HAD COME TO THE CANADIAN ARCTIC AS researchers with an ambitious schedule of fieldwork. Karen and Laura were completing PhDs on birds, and Bob Montgomerie, a professor from Queen's University, Ontario, was their advisor. The three of them spent a lot of time engaged in earnest discussions in the dining room in the hut.

My role was to help out with Karen's study of the breeding behaviour of rock ptarmigan (the 'p' is silent), a rotund, robust, pheasant-like bird found throughout the Arctic. Karen was the researcher, making observations and conducting experiments. Much of the routine field-work and logistics was the responsibility of Tarmo, our technician, fixer and general-everything person. I have met plenty of clever and inventive field biologists over the years, but none came close to Tarmo for ingenuity and sheer determination. No matter the problem, he could find a solution, often something rigged together out of whatever was lying around and, of course, lots of duct tape. It was Tarmo who took me out for a first look around that first afternoon. Or was it morning? Or late at night? It was impossible to be sure. And our watches were hidden beneath many layers of down-filled clothing.

With one of the flare guns attached to my backpack, I strode out with the group, away from the hut. It might have been towards the east, but compasses are dodgy this close to the magnetic north pole. Everyone else, who had been here numerous times, knew the general directions, but my geographic intuition – untrustworthy at the best of times – had no chance when the sun never rose or set. It simply circled overhead, rendering both direction and time elastic. Or perhaps immaterial. I realised that knowing something about where I was and when was reassuring. Not having knowledge of either was unsettling.

The landscape we walked through was almost completely snow covered, but this was changing fast. Where the snow had melted, dark patches of tundra appeared. On the tops of the slight rises, and on the numerous boulders scattered about, the snow was thin and transparent. In places, every step I took crunched through this surface layer, exposing the dense prostrate vegetation community beneath. What damage was I doing, I wondered. Simply walking around was changing the pristine appearance of the place, leaving horribly conspicuous footprints.

Tarmo sensed my unease.

'Don't worry about it. The snow will mostly be gone by the end of the week and so will those footprints. And the plants? Tough as rocks.' He pressed on, striding through the snow with determination, eager to see something ahead.

'This low, flat area is the lake – Sarcpa. It's still frozen and covered in snow, so it's hard to picture right now. But it's big and has a huge population of Arctic char, one of the few fishes found in these ultra-cold waters. When the ice melts and the river begins to flow, I'll be ready to catch a bunch.'

We stopped at a slight rocky rise and looked out over the landscape ahead. There were a few birds flitting about – mostly small and pale, and entirely disinterested in the newly arrived humans. The two main species were snow buntings, dirty-white soft-looking sprites fossicking for seeds among the patches of exposed tundra, and finch-like Lapland longspurs, who gathered around us fearlessly like sparrows scavenging for crumbs around the tables at a Montreal café. Both species were petite, light, seemingly fragile. You would think that any passing storm could blow them away. Yet here they were, having flown on tiny wings hundreds of kilometres from somewhere far to the south, just in time to start breeding.

Tarmo holds up his hand and then points towards a boulder a short distance away. I train my binoculars on the place he is indicating; a small cream-coloured bird is hopping confidently around newly exposed tundra plants in a small gap in the snow. It is carrying bits of dry grass and moss in its stout, seed-crushing bill. Then, with a sudden flutter, it disappears into a dark space beneath the boulder.

Tarmo beams. 'Just in time,' he says quietly, with evident relief. He looks at me expectantly.

'Nest building?' I venture, tentatively. I can't even pretend that I'm up to speed with my Arctic behavioural ecology.

'Of course! Which means …?'

'That's a male waiting for a mate?'

'Exactly. That's a male snow bunting. What's the date? Sixth of June? Yeah, that's about right. Just in time.'

The male emerges from the cavity and flies over to a patch of tundra a few metres away.

'Just in time for what, exactly?' I ask. There is no point in pretending to know more than I do.

'Oh, sorry,' said Tarmo. 'I forgot that precise migration schedules are not typical of Aussie birds. Just in time to establish their territories and build nests, ready for the females, who should get here tomorrow or the next day. June sixth it was, last year.'

Back in Toronto, I had learned that our fieldwork schedule had been timed very closely to that of the arrival times of the migratory birds we were going to be studying. It was almost unbelievable to me that they could be so accurate with the dates. When I'd explained that a typical breeding season for an Australian species was some-thing like, 'Oh, you know, sometime between May and

September, depending on the weather,' Tarmo was equally astonished. 'Aussie birds really are laid back, eh?' he had said at the time.

Tarmo returns to his theme. 'Just in time to find a mate,' he said, watching the busy male on the ground in front of us. 'Having a warm, safe nest will be exactly what a prospective mate will be looking for. Once they've paired up, the females need to prepare their bodies for laying eggs. They'll be obsessed with finding protein-rich food: mostly, insect larvae and some seeds. With the snow starting to melt in places, these bare spots will be ideal for foraging. Completely different to what the males found when they arrived.'

Tarmo explains that the males have already been here for a few weeks; in some cases, a month. The snow was only just thawing now. A month ago, the entire landscape would have still been covered in metres of snow.

'Male "snowflakes" – that's what everyone calls snow buntings – are probably the very first birds to arrive up here. The conditions can be terrible: violent storms, relentless winds, temperatures around minus 30 degrees Celcius. And somehow they find sufficient food – wind-blown seeds, dead insects, frozen caribou dung – and try to survive until the females arrive. It's a dangerous game, but clearly it must be worth it.'

Why risk this appalling hardship? What propels these tiny birds to travel so far, so early? Good places to breed seems to be the key reason. Once the spring kicks off and the snow disappears, the High Arctic can be a wonderful place to breed, as long as you can secure a good place for a nest. An ideal spot will be dry, sheltered and well hidden, safe from predators and easy to defend. Such places are in extremely high demand. Generations of competition has resulted in this hazardous arms race where males attempt to be the first to arrive and stake a claim. Those that survive will easily attract mates and have a much better chance of raising chicks successfully.

And the females also have to get their timing exactly right. Like everything else up here, it's fraught with risk. Too early and they won't have anywhere to breed. Nest sites need to be ice-free and have a nearby supply of the right sort of vegetation to provide an insulation layer between nest and the permanently frozen ground beneath. The females also need to recover from the exhausting journey they have just completed.

And they need to choose a mate. That's pretty easy if they are among the first females to arrive; there will be plenty of over-eager males spruiking their real estate. Too late and the only fellows left will the also-rans flogging damp, drafty nests open to the weather and visible to the hawks or foxes. The consequences of being late are far more serious than disgruntled mothers-in-law facing those still stuck in Toronto.

There is another timing factor that needs to be considered. In fact, it's the main reason so many species of birds make the incredibly risky journey all the way north to the High Arctic every year. It may sound trivial, but a dependable supply of baby food is one of the most important evolutionary factors for all birds. And that is almost exclusively insects. Whatever type of food adult birds may live on – fish, berries, fruit, leaves, nuts or seeds, like the snow buntings – all baby birds are raised on insects. How nestlings develop during their first few weeks will affect them for the rest of their lives. The rapidly growing nestlings are ferociously hungry, demanding a constant supply of high-quality protein. And that is usually found in the form of insect larvae.

Everywhere, breeding birds have timed their breeding timetable so that the hatching of their ravenous offspring coincides with the maximum supply of insects. Get that wrong and the whole system can fall apart. It's one of the reasons the breeding schedules of these Arctic migrants are so strict. Every pair of buntings will be counting on a good supply of insects for their nestlings; if it all goes according to plan, their babies should have a steady supply of black fly grubs in about four weeks' time.

It's not just Arctic migrants whose activities are planned around black fly emergence. Our departure is timed primarily to avoid these minute blood-sucking menaces. What draws untold millions of birds to the High Arctic annually also drives humans to flee and the resident mammals mad. The sheer abundance of these insects is almost impossible to comprehend.

*Bob has given us a day off. We've been working for twelve days straight, so it's a welcome change to our routine. Tarmo and Karen grab their fishing gear and head straight over to the now rapidly flowing torrent emerging from beneath the lake to see how many Arctic char they can land. This too is an earnest competition. The others are celebrating by staying in bed and reading, or catching up on chores. I'm going for a long walk to do a bit of birdwatching. I know that's what I do every day, but this isn't 'work' birdwatching. And I'm going in a completely new direction for a change. Tarmo said he had seen a parasitic jaeger, a brutally efficient avian predator, a few kilometres to the west, hunting the longspur fledglings that seem to be everywhere at the moment. I've never seen a jaeger, so it's worth a try.*

Birding here is completely different. There aren't a lot of species, but those that do travel all the way up here do so in extraordinary numbers. And new ones seem to be appearing daily. Yesterday, an enormous flock of snow geese – ivory white, with bullet-shaped bodies and long, outstretched necks – passed low overhead before disappearing into the glare. Their honking added a new earthy element to the increasingly complex soundtrack. Mostly there is so little sound that every noise – and they are almost all bird calls – seem like an additional bright pattern of colour being embroidered onto the backdrop of silence.

*What was that? A shadow passed close to my right shoulder, but without the slightest sound. There! It swooped and landed on a tall dark boulder just ahead. Oh wow, is it …? It's just a white blob by eye, but through the binoculars it glows like polished marble. A snowy owl! My first. It's glaring directly at me with brutal power and arrogant ease. Completely at home here. Look at those eyes. Like yellow lasers.*
  *Wait, something's moving in the background.*

*I look up and am momentarily confused. Much of the landscape behind the owl is pulsating and fragmenting. It's in the direction of the dull sun, which is low in the silver, glary sky. I scan with my binoculars and finally make out shapes. Large, mottled, faded browns and greys amid the usual white.*

*And then I hear something. Muffled low grunts, growls, snorts. Barely discernible but an entirely new sound.*

*Caribou! Maybe thirty or so. It's hard to pick out individuals as they blend so well into the now mottled patchwork landscape. I'm surprised to see such large animals here. The snow geese have been the biggest so far.*

*The caribou seem restless. Spooked. Pretty sure it's not because of me, but I'm a little unsettled myself. I decide to head back.*

'IT'S STALKIN' PTARMIE TIME,' DECLARES KAREN.

Rock ptarmigan are the main reason I'm here after all, to assist Karen with her project. Knowing my interest in bird breeding behaviour, her advisor, Bob Montgomerie, had invited me to join his research group on their annual Arctic expedition.

'Enough of those little feathered things,' she says. 'Let's show you a real tundra bird.' Tarmo shoulders his bulging backpack, stuffed with all sorts of equipment – including a flare gun – and hands me a strange aluminium cylinder that is about 2 metres long. When I look puzzled, he says, 'Don't worry. I'll explain soon.' Karen carries a smaller canvas bag.

Rock ptarmigan are *the* quintessential Arctic bird. No other species lives permanently in the tundra, only moving south a little to avoid the perpetual darkness of midwinter. When the light returns, these dumpy, chicken-like birds return every year to breed during the few snow-free weeks of mid-summer. 'And they literally return to right *here*,' Karen explains as we trudge towards the first breeding grounds to be occupied. 'Most of the males settle onto exactly the same patch they had in previous years.' This landscape might seem featureless to us, but the birds know exactly where they are.

Like the buntings, male ptarmigan arrive just before the females, in order to claim a patch of tundra. The females will be here within days, and tensions are high, both for the birds, who are fighting over territories, and for us, who will be trying to catch as many as we can before the females arrive. Yes, catch. That's where my aluminium cylinder comes in.

We pause at a slight rise that overlooks an area that to me looks exactly the same as everywhere else. Possibly there are a few more patches of brown tundra in the monotonous snowfields than elsewhere.

'This is prime ptarmie real estate,' Karen says, scanning the surroundings through her binoculars. 'Less snow means more places for the females to set up nest sites. Now, let's see if you can spot any males. They'll only be on the snowy parts, trying to blend in. Look for something white.'

We laugh.

I raise my binoculars and begin scanning the

undulating slopes in front of me. Almost instantly I see something move against the grey-blue sky: two white blobs rise and collide in the air before separating and gliding back to earth. They vanish against the snow, so I focus on the spot where the closest one seemed to have landed.

Even without the binoculars I can make out a rotund, gleaming white body against the mottled grey-white snow. It's only about 30 metres away. We intuitively freeze. I have no idea what is supposed to happen now, but Tarmo does.

Keeping a close eye on the ptarmigan – who completely ignores us and keeps cocking his head towards the sky – Tarmo takes the aluminium cylinder and begins to extend it. It's a cleverly designed telescopic apparatus, with multiple sections fitting neatly together. Fully extended it becomes a pole about 6 metres long with a loop of cord at the tip.

'Tarmo and I are both pretty darned good at this rather specialised skill,' whispers Karen excitedly. 'I'm letting Tarmo have the first attempt so I can explain what's happening. But have no doubt: this is a deadly serious competition. I beat him by three last year, so he's out to prove a point!'

Tarmo is already moving stealthily in the general direction of the ptarmigan, bent low and holding the pole close to the ground. The bird notices the unfamiliar figure, but as it seems to be walking past, he loses interest and continues to scan the air above.

'The trick is to pretend you aren't interested in them,' explains Karen. 'You can see Tarmo is making it look like he's concentrating on something to one side. Most rock ptarmigan never see humans, so they aren't too concerned. Still, all animals get uneasy if they think they're being stared at.'

Tarmo is now about 10 metres from the bird. Facing about forty-five degrees to the left but keeping him in his peripheral vision, Tarmo gently swings the pole towards the male. The end is only about 2 metres from the bird. Gingerly, Tarmo moves closer, the pole now almost at the bird's head height. It still appears not to have noticed anything alarming. Even more astonishing, Tarmo is managing to keep the very long, thin, unstable pole almost perfectly still.

Ever so carefully, Tarmo tilts the pole slightly and deftly drops the loop of cord over the bird's head. Nearly there ... Got him!

There is an instant reaction from both Tarmo and Karen: both move towards the bird as fast as heavy boots and bulging backpacks will allow. The bird is thrashing about on the end of the pole, uttering guttural grunts of alarm. As he closes in on the bird, Tarmo extracts a large cloth bag he had earlier stuffed into a jacket pocket. With the apparent ease that comes with lots of practice, he drops to his knees and deftly envelops the bird in the bag. Cradling the moving, squawking bundle to his chest with his right arm, he inserts his left hand into the bag, feeling his way with his fingers to unloop the cord from around the bird's neck. All the while he has been quietly offering reassurance to his victim: 'Sorry about this, buddy. Yeah, I know. It sucks. But you'll be free very soon.'

'Don't they bite?' I ask.

'They never do,' says Karen. 'It's strange. They could do some real damage with that strong bill, but they don't. It's one of the reasons I love these guys.'

The main reason for catching this bird – and others over the next few days – is to turn a generic male rock ptarmigan, identical to all the others, into a recognisable individual. Recognisable to us, that is. The birds know who's who, but humans need something conspicuous that can be seen from afar. Being able to distinguish each bird is essential if Karen is to make sense of their movements and interactions. Are the same birds mating up again this year? Has each male reclaimed his favourite spot, or has a younger, fitter – or simply earlier – rival taken his place? These questions can only be answered if you can reliably recognise individuals.

The standard method of marking most birds is to attach coloured bands to their legs. These are harmless plastic rings in a range of colours that are visible from a distance. The bands retain their colour for years and plenty of the male ptarmigan we saw were wearing leg bands. These ones didn't need to be caught again.

Tarmo gently hands me the squirming bag and prepares the equipment. I sit on the cold, damp rock and cradle the bird on my crossed legs. Each time a part of the bird is required I feel around inside the bag with one hand and try to locate the required wing, head or leg so that it can be temporarily exposed for examination. As Tarmo completes each measurement, he states the number. Karen repeats it, and Tarmo confirms the figure. Checking like this is essential, to ensure the records are reliable. All the usual things are measured – weight (suspending the bird and bag from a small spring balance), wing length, beak width and length.

There is one ptarmigan-specific measure as well: the length and size and colour of the vivid red comb, a fleshy, flexible protuberance above the eye. This is the only part of the bird's anatomy that isn't white. Karen is interested in whether the comb plays a role in a female's mate choice. (It does, as she discovered; bigger and redder is much more attractive!)

Fitting the leg bands is the final indignity. Karen attaches three bands: two on the left leg and one on the right. She has a quaint tradition: the first male of the year, formally – and boringly – known as blue-red-blue, is also given a name. This one, they announce, is to be called 'Ozzie', in honour of possibly the first (only?) Australian to have ever handled a rock ptarmigan.

Processing complete (in under ten minutes), I place the bag on the ground, open it fully and step back. There is a moment of hesitation as Ozzie's head protrudes from the folds of cloth and he looks around with a thoroughly annoyed expression. Then, in a blur of wings, he rockets off just above the surface, and lands on a boulder about 20 metres away. He turns and directs a torrent of harsh coarse grating sounds toward us.

Ozzie is the first of about a dozen males we are able to catch and mark over the following weeks. They join those already marked on previous years to enable us to start our observations in earnest. According to Karen, we have about three days in total before the first females arrive. Our urgent task is to determine which males have settled where, and compare the pattern to previous years. This is something I can start right away while the others concentrate on more capture and marking. It is vital to get as many males banded as soon as possible. I leave them to it.

That afternoon, I start a long, slow walk through the area Karen refers to as Ptarmie Heights, a slightly raised series of slopes the birds, for whatever reason, regard as the best places.

It takes a while to get my eye in, as they say. Again, it is the old problem of trying to see white objects against the vast white landscape. That scenery is, however, changing rapidly. With every passing day, more and more patches of dark green tundra appear and expand as the snow cover steadily diminishes. For the all-white male ptarmigan, this poses an existential challenge: to stay hidden from predators they need to remain on the snowy places. At these latitudes, bullet-shaped gyrfalcon are an ever-present and lethal threat. Of the several birds of prey in the area, these are the most stealthy, moving so fast they are almost impossible to see.

Being able to blend into the background really is a matter of life and death. By the end of June – in about two weeks' time – there will be no snow at all, and rather than perfect camouflage, the ptarmigans' whiteness will become a deadly liability. Once the entire landscape is the dark mottled tartan of the tundra, there will be literally nowhere to hide.

Of course, for the soon-but-not-too-soon-to-arrive

females, the loss of the snow cover is what they are hoping for. It would be hard to imagine a better match between bird and background than a female rock ptarmigan hunkered down in the tundra hiding her precious eggs. Their plumage is composed of the mottled shades of moss, lichen and dead leaves. They aren't so much 'well hidden' as completely invisible. Several times I saw a female fly in and settle onto her nest only a short distance away. I tried to focus on the exact place she had landed and crept stealthily towards the spot. The only time I successfully found one was when I stepped on her back. She gave a slight exasperated wheeze and glared fiercely at me as I apologised. She didn't move, trusting her camouflage was working as intended.

After we have carefully mapped where the males have been settling, it becomes clear to Karen that something is not right. She scrutinises her records repeatedly, a concerned expression on her face. When I return late one afternoon to report no further males have shown up, she looks genuinely alarmed.

'What on earth has happened to the males!' she says quietly, gazing at the large map on which all the birds' location are being recorded.

The first females are appearing and are busy selecting nest sites, yet many of the males' traditional territories remain unoccupied. These areas have been mapped and monitored by a sequence of researchers for years. Some of the males who owned them had become well known; their arrival dates, territory boundaries and various individual quirks were all highly predictable. (One male, Pierre –

or purple-green-blue – took a liking to Tarmo and would walk towards him whenever he was passing through.) Yet too many – including Pierre – were no-shows. By 25 June, when most of the females have completed their clutch of between two and a dozen eggs and are busy incubating, almost half of the population of males has failed to appear.

THIS IS A CATASTROPHIC DISRUPTION OF WHAT IS usually a well-oiled and predictable reproductive system, honed by the severe conditions to be as efficient as possible. It has to be. The timing has to be precise and reliable. All Arctic residents know the consequences of getting it wrong.

The typical territorial scenario among the males is intense jostling for a few days as they test their territory boundaries. Where a dispute over space is severely contested, violent physical clashes can erupt. These birds may look round and soft, but feathers fly and bodies often slam together repeatedly until one retreats. It is hard to imagine any real damage being done, but the conspicuous comb is an obvious target. A number of males carry the visible scars of past battles.

After a few days of testosterone-driven posturing and pouting among the males, everything changes dramatically when the females suddenly turn up. A frantic realignment of priorities from geography to proximity. The females settle on the same location as they have done previously, thereby becoming the mate of the male already occupying the site. They have an important job to do and there is no time to lose.

Over the first week or so, the couples are rarely more than a metre apart. This is no 'can't keep their hands off one another' scenario; it's effectively obsessive stalking by the overly clingy males. It's a behaviour known as mate-guarding. The females ovulate only once over a few days each year, the only time mating can result in fertilisation. The male's possessiveness ensures that no other male can try anything with their mate. It all works smoothly because everyone knows the rules and the geography. Typically, this almost always means a nice suburban nuclear family equivalent, with one female residing in the territory of one male. And it's usually going to be the same two individuals.

Such domestic reliability is out the window this year. Literally half the normal number of males has turned up, meaning the territories are much bigger this season. The females, in contrast, have returned in the same numbers as previously. When they have all found their usual patch, the males discover several females have settled in *their* patch. That might sound like a lot of fun, but for the normally monogamous rock ptarmigan, it is thoroughly disconcerting.

Instead of being able to relax with their territorial boundaries confirmed, the males find themselves frantic-ally crisscrossing their expanded territories every time they see or even suspect another male crossing the boundary. Mate-guarding becomes frantic and frustrating. It is exhausting even to watch. And given the twenty-four hours of daytime, there is no downtime. The irony of all this action by the males is that it is largely futile. There are no unmated females to fret over. Virtually all of them have already mated with whoever the local male is, and are ensconced on their well-concealed nests, sensibly leaving the boys to their pointless assertiveness.

Futile, perhaps, but it is as though they have to keep up the pretence of vigilance against trespassers, even when it makes little sense. As we continue our routine observations, the cost of this unexpected additional effort becomes noticeable. We increasingly notice exhausted males, bedraggled and thin, sheltering out of sight behind boulders. Instead of foraging for most of the day, they are engaged in constant flying and fighting, and rarely getting the chance to replenish their energy reserves. The risks are all too obvious. The Arctic foxes, in particular, seem well aware of their vulnerability. Normally, a male will rocket into the air as soon as a fox comes anywhere near them. As the season wears on, however, the males seem reluctant to fly, or are simply exhausted. The results are all too evident: sad piles of bloody white feathers.

'Another one,' laments Tarmo one day towards the end of our trip. He is probing his gloved fingers through another mound of feathers and finds what he hopes he won't: a short, feathered leg with two coloured leg bands still attached. 'Blue-blue' – probably green on the other leg. 'This was Jean-Marc, the oldest bird in this location, probably banded five years ago.' He places the leg in a zip-lock bag and shakes his head.

'This has been the worst year for predation we've ever seen. And that's on top of whatever catastrophe happened to the males before they even got here. It's just as well the females don't need the males to help raise the kids.'

'The foxes are having a great time, on the other hand,' he added. 'I've never seen so many out and about.' He pauses, looking intently off towards the horizon.

I follow the direction of his gaze. There is something, a long way off. 'Wrong shape for a fox, but I can't tell how big it is,' Tarmo says. I see him reaching behind to make sure the flare gun is still attached to the side of his backpack.

We raise our binoculars at the same time and try to focus on the distant object. It is white and roundish, not elongated like a fox. Believe it or not, even though it is probably only about 7 degrees Celsius, a shimmering heat haze rises from the tundra, making it a little harder to get a clear view. I feel my heart beat faster.

And then it raises its head. We see two sharp ears attached to an almost spherical ball of fur. 'It's a bunny,' says Tarmo, with a mixture of relief and delight. 'An Artic hare. World's largest lagomorph. I think we're safe.' And we both laugh loudly.

We did see a polar bear, on the way home. It was a pelt, attached to a washing line in a backyard back at Sanirajak. 'More and more bears coming into town now,' explained a resident when we asked about the skin. 'No seals any more. Too little ice. The bears come now to eat rubbish.'

IN 1989, WHEN THIS ADVENTURE TOOK PLACE, 'climate change' and 'global warming' were terms little known outside universities and weather bureaus. The Inuit of the Canadian Arctic knew something was happening.

The ice thaw was starting earlier, the seals were harder to catch, and there were years when the nestlings of the coastal seabirds that once roosted in their millions along the cliffs starved to death.

Even back then, as the threads of the great tapestry of biodiversity were starting to fray, very few people noticed. It was old-fashioned naturalists who documented the dates of first flowering, the first appearance of hibernating hedgehogs or the arrival of migratory birds, recorded methodically in hundreds of notebooks. It wasn't until some prescient researchers began to compile these private records and compare these dates going back centuries that the first hints of an alarming vision became apparent: a slow but definite unravelling. The exquisitely interwoven connections between all the species that make up every ecosystem were starting to separate.

But why? Surely nature had not stopped adapting to change. Millennia of intricate interactions, fine-tuned to functional perfection, had created a self-correcting system that thrived on variability and prospered when challenged by random events. A wildfire, a cyclone, an epidemic, a prolonged drought – all sharpened the blades of natural selection and honed the whole to be profoundly resilient. Variability led to essential pruning. Every element in the multidimensional mosaic shifted and adjusted as required.

Until the changes became too big, too often and too fast. The effects we see everywhere in the world today began to impact the polar regions earlier than elsewhere. When cold and frozen are the norm, planet-wide warming is going to be especially noticeable. Here, the timing of arrivals and departures of birds, egg-laying and the feeding of young, flowering cycles and the emergence of their pollinators, the rousing of hibernators, the moulting and shedding of winter's white plumage and pelage for tundra-themed summer alternatives – all were changing.

# (3)
## WHEN the HUNTER DIDN'T

WE HAVE BEEN STRUGGLING UP THIS SLOPE FOR hours. I'd told the students to be prepared for a gruelling trek; they probably thought I was exaggerating. 'It's going to be a tough climb,' I explained the day before. 'It's slippery and treacherous. You'll be exhausted and covered in mud. And leeches.' I didn't want anyone to feel that they had been misled about the challenge they faced. And I made it clear that there was no compulsion to come. Yet when I asked who wanted to come, everyone raised a hand.

It's early the next day. We are on a steep mountainside, deep in the interior of Borneo. Dense tropical rainforest surrounds us, restricting the view to a few metres. The air is as warm and moist as a sauna; every breath seems inadequate. There's not a hint of a breeze, no relief from the oppressive humidity. Every part of every body is wringing wet. Water bottles are more and more frequently guzzled; will there be any left for the trip back down?

With us are several local guides, one with the small group up the front and two following close behind. We might be wheezing and wringing wet but they haven't stopped chatting, laughing or smoking the whole time. Despite their apparent nonchalance, they keep a very close eye on us. Twice now, someone has stumbled or tripped; a guide instantly appeared beside them, reassuring and gently assisting. Knowing these calm, professionally trained guides are with us is reassuring. I'm supposed to be in charge, but can do little more than decide where to place my next step.

After a few hours, the fatigue is beginning to show. There is more stumbling, mumbling, swearing. Tripping on exposed roots. Grabbing a vine in desperation, and discovering too late it's covered in sharp spines. Occasionally someone tries a futile attempt to motivate: 'Nearly there!', 'Let's go, everyone!', 'It will be so worth it!'. Then 'Whose idea was *this*?'

The reason for all this effort? And risk? Put simply, we are looking for a decent view. A place high up on this oddly shaped mountain range where we can see for ourselves why it is called 'Maliau *Basin*'. We're trying to reach the rim of this colossal crater-like formation to see beyond the closed curtain of the rainforest that surrounds us back at the research station.

In late June 2019, about 20 undergraduate students and a few university staff flew to Borneo to participate in a course of the ecology of tropical rainforest. I had been running this event for almost a decade. As normal, for many of the students, this was their first time out of Australia. We had landed in Kota Kinabalu, the capital of Sabah, the Malaysian state that covers the top third of Borneo. We spent a day getting used to the humidity and goading each other into tasting some of the exotic foods available in the markets. Everyone was expected to try the infamously odorous fruit known as durian ('smells like fermented football socks but tastes like custard' is one of the more polite versions of the experience). The following day, we boarded several minibuses and spent most of the day driving into the heart of northern Borneo.

We arrived at the Maliau Basin Studies Centre late in the day. It's a modern facility set up primarily for researchers to investigate aspects of this tropical rainforest. Tourists are welcome, but it is so remote that relatively few make it this far inland. Maliau's companion facilities, the famous Danum Valley Field Centre and Borneo Rainforest Lodge, are much more accessible and have many more visitors.

The remoteness is fine with us. We're here to immerse ourselves in the place and to make the most of what is likely to be a once-in-a-lifetime experience. The students cycle through a series of projects: counting birds, collecting butterflies and dragonflies, setting up camera surveys, recording bat calls, and other activities. These are the planned, organised components of the course, but virtually every day something remarkable and unexpected happens. A group of muddy bearded pigs might suddenly emerge from the jungle and charge past, oblivious to the gaping people nearby. A pair of rhinoceros hornbills fly ponderously past, their weird otherworldly calls echoing through the valley. On every trip, an exceptionally rare or elusive animal is encountered: a colugo, a huge gliding mammal, sleeping on an exposed tree trunk; a pair of Bornean ground-cuckoos snatching insects disturbed by foraging sun bears. Once, incredibly, a clouded leopard, possibly the rarest mammal in South-East Asia, pausing briefly while crossing the road only a few metres from us. But even the regular, routine things seem somehow magical. Every morning, we are roused from sleep by the echoing hoots of the gibbons, loudly broadcasting their presence to the waking world.

At the research station and on all excursions into the forest, we are surrounded closely by dense, towering rainforest trees. The Bornean rainforest has the highest canopy in the world, on average about 50 metres above the ground. Even more spectacular are the 'emergents' – exceptionally tall trees that extend far above the canopy. One such tree was recently discovered to be the tallest tropical tree in the world: a staggering 101 metres high.

But despite the excitement of exploring this extra-ordinary place, there is also an undeniable feeling of being closed in, almost claustrophobically. It's impossible to visualise the broader landscape. With each day spent on the floor of the basin, the yearning to see it from above – to take in the shape and scale of the massive structure that surrounds us but can't be seen – becomes something of an obsession. Of course, we have all scrutinised the Google Earth images, but that is not very satisfactory. They show the basin as a roughly circular shape, slightly darker green than the surrounding forest, but the images are grainy and give no impression of the terrain.

There is a much more 'concrete' way to envisage the landform. In front of the main administration building is a large concrete model of the Maliau Basin. It's pretty crude, but shows the general shape of the terrain. It is a roughly circular massif with extremely steep outer walls and a deeply depressed centre. Indeed, it does look like a basin, although 'bowl' would also work. It looks for all the world like a crater formed by a sizeable meteorite, or possibly a broad, collapsed volcanic caldera. But it is neither.

Instead of a cataclysmic cosmic collision or geothermal activity, the processes that created the basin were much more prosaic: eons of rain and erosion. The local rocks are mainly shallow sea sediments. In the very distant past, a vast block of these had been raised thousands of metres by monumental seismic pressures, and was then sculpted and scoured by relentless erosion. It helped to be in one of the wettest places on earth. So no dramatic origin story, but the effect is no less stunning.

The model is fairly accurate, although the vertical scale has clearly been exaggerated for dramatic effect. Key places and walking trails have been painted on at various locations. A red dot indicates 'You Are Here', showing the cluster of buildings just outside the basin, close to where the Maliau River emerges through the only gap in the surrounding walls. A thin blue line – a road – arcs away from the station then curves back towards the basin, finishing at the base of its southern edge. The green dot is Agathis Camp, a series of huts at the start of a walking trail. A pale yellow line crawls vertically up the impossibly steep slope before flattening out along the rim. 'Yes. That's the spot,' I think to myself. 'Surely that's where we'll get a view of the whole place.'

There is no other option; we have to walk up to this place on the rim and see for ourselves.

On the day of the climb, we rise early and pile into several of the station's four-wheel drives. About an hour later, we assemble at Agathis Camp to start our walk. The rudimentary trail becomes extremely steep almost immediately and remains so for almost the entire climb. During the many necessary rest stops, someone would draw attention to a bizarre fungus or weird beetle. Ear-piercingly loud cicadas, sounding like monstrous dentist's drills or angle grinders, screech at intervals. Strange bird calls echo in the distance, but the birds are almost never seen. Not that anyone is taking any notice; we are all focused intently on where to place the next step.

'Imagine trying to climb down in the dark,' someone says, panting and leaning against a wet tree trunk.

'Imagine doing this in the rain,' I say. As if on cue, thunder rumbles ominously from somewhere behind us. It is a powerful incentive to keep moving. We all know how heavy and sudden a downpour can be. Being caught out on these already treacherous slopes is not something we want to experience.

Maliau Basin, stretching as it does along the northern part of Borneo, is one of the wettest places in Asia, receiving over 4 metres of rain annually. Most of this is dumped during the two annual wet seasons, August–September and November–December. The locals tell you there are three likely weather forecasts in Borneo: wet, really wet, and really *really* wet. In other words: expect rain. Anytime. And definitely do not get caught out on a steep, slippery slope during a downpour! Even when the terrain is flat and the weather dry, walking safely here requires concentration. Walking down a very steep slope is always risky, but in the rain …

After some hours of clambering slowly up the very steep slopes, the trail becomes literally vertical. Several aluminium ladders with treacherously slippery rungs have been lashed to trees and roots to enable climbing. It is slow, exhausting work. Conversations stop. Everyone is exhausted.

Suddenly the trail levels out and widens. The structure of the forest becomes noticeably different to that of the steep slopes we have just passed through. The trees are larger and the canopy denser, but there is less understorey. We have reached the rim of the basin but the jungle is still too dense to see far. We need to find that place on the very inner edge.

With new-found enthusiasm, we pick up the pace and follow the trail towards the west. In places, we are walking on the sharp edge of the rim, only half a metre wide. To the left, the land vanishes precipitously. Slip here and you won't stop until whatever is left of you reaches the bottom. The slope to the right recedes more gently away towards the centre of the basin. In a few places, however, the trail seemed to follow a knife-edge rim, the land disappearing sharply down either side. Progress here requires concentration, each step to be taken cautiously.

'HEY. HERE IT IS! YOU CAN SEE EVERY-THING!'

Someone up ahead is shouting. Those of us at the back

of the queue find some enthusiasm and pick up speed. We follow the chorus of excited voices wafting through the trees. All signs of exhaustion and frustration have disappeared. We join the group on the very edge of a sheer cliff that vanishes vertically a few metres from where we stand. The spirited banter subsides as everyone pauses to take in the extraordinary scene before us.

Far below us, the floor of the basin is a vast, slightly undulating landscape of rich, dark green spread lumpily all the way to the sheer walls on the far side, about 25 kilometres away. The rim is a rich, jagged boundary between land and sky, obscured in places by dense cloud spilling silently over the rim like whipped cream being poured into a bowl. Everywhere, tendrils and lagoons of silvery mist flow imperceptibly, filling depressions in the landscape or rising like smoke from a cigar. It is quiet, but not silent: muffled bird calls and gibbon hoots float up from somewhere far below. The distance makes it impossible to make out any details, but the entire landscape is unbroken, uninterrupted, untouched – tropical rainforest, complete and intact.

No one speaks for quite a while. We are lost in our private thoughts, seemingly transfixed by the colossal scene we are taking in. This vast landscape, in every direction, is entirely natural. There is literally no visible sign of human activity. There are not many places on the planet that can make that claim. It makes the difficult journey to get here thoroughly worthwhile.

BEARDED PIGS TEND TO BE THE FIRST WILD ANIMALS we see upon arrival at the Maliau Basin Study Centre. And it's not the brief, furtive glimpse typical of a sambar deer or civet sighting before they disappear into the forest. As likely as not, several pigs will be wandering past or lounging in the shade when the vehicles arrive. Typically, they will look up with a gaze of studied indifference, or possibly naked contempt. Some may even slowly approach – not in a threatening manner, simply curious to see whether this group of humans is worth investigating. What is perfectly plain to even the most inattentive is that we are temporary visitors to their domain, and we had best remember that.

When twenty-something Alex stepped out of the minibus and gazed around in wonder, the first thing she saw was Boris. He stood a short distance away, his tiny black eyes scanning this latest set of intruders. And then he saw her. She was definitely the most beautiful human he had ever seen. For Alex, Boris was definitely the most hideously grotesque creature she had ever seen. His coarse scrappy beard was matted with mud and dead leaves. His muscular torso was a patchwork of uneven, bristly hair. He seemed to be grinning, a lop-sided grimace that was creepy and endearing. She couldn't take her eyes off him.

'He had a lovely wrinkly back,' she told me recently, her thoughts drifting back to that magical moment, 'so I called him Wrinkles.'

Boris/Wrinkles spent most of the day beneath the dormitory building occupied by the female students. That way he could be close to his beloved when she was there. He didn't accompany her on her daily trips into the rainforest, but was content to wait patiently for her return. When some women's underwear disappeared from the washing line, Wrinkles was the leading suspect. 'But where's the proof?' Alex demanded when the accusations started. 'Just because he's a pig, doesn't mean he's a "pig"!'

The students were already feeling unsettled by the disappearance of some chocolate biscuits from under a bed in the dorm. *That* culprit was caught red-handed late one night. A beautiful but brazen Malay civet was busted, exiting stealthily through a door left open by someone heading to the toilet. There he was, frozen in the glare of several phone lights. 'He didn't even look guilty!' said Alex. 'He stood still for a moment, a Tim Tam clamped between his teeth, before bolting out the door in a flash. I suggested that this might have been the undies thief, but no one believed me.'

Bearded pigs, solitary or in small groups, wander freely about the grassy surroundings of the centre's buildings, or snooze under the numerous raised walkways. Younger animals of either sex usually move about in small groups. The older males – who can weigh up to a massive 200 kilograms – are normally solitary and constantly displace any lower-ranked males they encounter, grunting with belligerence. Sows with litters of up to a dozen chocolate-striped piglets – the only phase in their lives where they could be regarded as cute – usually remain hidden in the rainforest, well away from the testosterone-powered dramas of the males.

All pig species have oversized, triangular heads, but the

bearded's is the largest of them all. The snout is impressively long, but what draws your attention is the huge, unkempt 'beard' of thick, elongated bristles that encircles the snout like a mop. This beard hair is, apparently, white, but as they spend most of their time snuffling about the muddy forest floor, it is usually the colour of the local soil, and matted with soil, grass and leaves.

Now who am I to question evolution's wisdom, but frankly, it's hard to see the utility of this feature. It's always a mess and must obscure their view, but to a mammal so obviously 'led by the nose', perhaps that doesn't matter. The reality is that no one is entirely sure what function the beard serves. Like so much about these fascinating and important animals, very little has been investigated in detail. Only the barest rudiments of their behaviour and ecological role have been studied and, as we will see, that may be a serious problem.

It may seem strange to highlight a humble pig as the focus of this story from Borneo. There are plenty of other likely contenders. In terms of beauty, perhaps the clouded leopard; conservation, the Sumatran rhinoceros; or cultural importance, the rhinoceros hornbill. But none come close in terms of overall significance to Borneo as a whole. In the words of Quentin Phillips, the renowned British and Borneo-raised naturalist and author, 'The bearded pig is by far the most important mammal in Bornean forests.' The indigenous people refer to the species as 'the gardeners of the forest', attributing them with literally designing the rainforest through their activities.

We will explore why this species means so much, both ecologically and culturally, at least within the limitations of what is known.

GURONG IS AN ELDER OF THE INDIGENOUS Kadazandusun-Murut people who live along the Kinabatangan River, about 350 kilometres to the north-east. He is a cultural leader of his people. He is trying to describe what he saw.

We are sitting on the raised wooden deck next to the dining hall at the Maliau Basin Centre. I have invited him to the station to talk with the students about his life living in the rainforest. Our iced lime drinks ('limau') have long since reverted to the ambient temperature (about 32 degrees Celsius) as what I thought was a simple conversation-starter – 'Why are bearded pigs so important?' – turns into a long and moving consideration of his life and culture. Quietly spoken and reserved, Gurong is even more reticent after hearing my question. He is silent for some time, perhaps wondering how much to divulge to a complete and ignorant stranger. He sighs before saying: 'Okay, I will tell you what is important about these animals. But first, I must tell you about a time long ago. What I saw when I was in the forest, hunting.'

Gurong describes sitting quietly in a hunter's platform, a taut mat of woven vines, secured between tree trunks several metres above the forest floor. Below was a well-used passageway through the jungle used by many species. Gurong was waiting for tonight's dinner. Something suitable such as a deer or pheasant, or possibly a porcupine. He waited, listening intently, his sharp hearing alert to the smallest sound.

What Gurong heard, still some distance away, was very strange. He had spent most of his life in this forest. but had never heard anything like this. 'Like wind or rumbling. Like thunder,' he says, becoming increasingly animated. 'Was it an earthquake? I was now worried. Had I upset the forest spirits? Should I leave?'

Too late; whatever it was was close now, and coming fast. He waited apprehensively as the immense noise grew steadily louder. Now he could hear squeals and grunts amidst the dull rumbling.

And then they appeared.

'It was an army of babi hutan [bearded pigs]! But many. No could count. TOO MANY!'

A tsunami of pigs – thousands, it seemed. A vast, fast-moving swarm, running in tight formation. The entire forest floor became a mass of surging, muddy grey bodies, accompanied by continuous grunting, squealing and an occasional full-throated roar. But they weren't disturbed or panicky.

'They were busy, going somewhere; they knew where. They were excited and focused. I was amazed! Shocked. I felt happy to see them. But also worried. What did it mean? What should I do?'

Gurong says he failed in his duties as a hunter that day, but did so for the right reasons. His family were expecting him to return with tonight's meat. Babi is always the favourite. And all these pigs directly below were more than he had imagined existed in the entire world! But this was not a moment for hunting. It was about more than him simply obtaining food. He could not fire his rifle into the herd right in front of him. That would have been easy. But it wasn't right, he said. 'I am pig hunter, yes?' he says proudly, thumbing his chest. 'To hunt well you must train and learn. How to be careful, quiet, patient. I am very good hunter. Know how to stalk, very slowly, getting close before shooting.'

Killing the selected victim must be instant: a single, perfectly aimed shot. This is the only way. Firing blindly into a large herd is completely unacceptable. The pigs would have panicked. The forest spirits would then have been very angry. No, this huge herd was engaged in something out of the ordinary. He had seen migrating groups before, many times. He had been involved in hunts at well-known river crossings where the animals were forced to move in single file through a narrow canyon. Specific pigs could then be selected: big, robust, healthy males were the best. Spears were still being used in those situations.

Again, he tries to convey just how many pigs he had seen, but words fail him. He extends his arms to their widest span, saying in a low, awe-filled voice, 'So so many. Too too many to count!'

Once again, he becomes quiet and introspective. 'But that was my only time. Once in my life. Nothing that many since. Nothing like it.' His emotions have swung from the ecstasy of witnessing the event to the sobering reality that such a sight may never be witnessed again. It is an abrupt return to reality.

GURONG HAD BEEN A YOUNG MAN IN THE EARLY 1980s when he witnessed that mass migration of bearded pigs near the Kinabatangan River in north-eastern Borneo. The number of animals in that migration was estimated by several observers to have been about a million, but it's impossible to be accurate. Certainly, no herds of that scale have been reported since. Bearded pig migrations still occur, irregularly as always and with a lot fewer animals. And that worries Gurong, for many reasons. Again, he is quiet and reflective.

Then our conversation is disrupted by a ferocious fracas on the ground below. An enormous male bearded pig has burst out of the nearby wall of rainforest. Roaring with menace, he charges into the open, scattering a group of younger males in all directions. And we soon see why. The people in the kitchen have just discarded the morning's vegetable scraps over the balcony onto the grassy area below. This is a daily ritual and 'the Boss' (as he is known) has arrived right on time. The displaced younger animals stand uneasily a safe distance away, as this huge, clearly dominant male – almost certainly their father – noisily scoffs the sweet potato peelings and rotten bananas.

Gurong watches with a serious expression. Shaking his head, he says, 'Look at him. Is sad to see big Boss tame. He should be in the jungle, digging for acorns and worms. He has become a pet. No good.'

I had felt something similar when I first noticed the Boss hanging around the dining hall. It seemed unseemly that the area's dominant male was scavenging discarded scraps instead of contributing to his species' critical ecological role in the rainforest. All pig species disturb the surface of the ground as they root around with their powerful snouts, overturning the upper soil layers, often over large areas, searching for food. Everything even vaguely edible is consumed, including seedlings and germinating fruit. This can be destructive – in places where the pigs remain for extended times, no young plants survive. But the soil churning is also vital in breaking up the humus layer, burying seeds and fruit and inadvertently encouraging certain plants to germinate.

Animals that have large-scale impacts on landscapes are known as ecosystem engineers. In the forests of Borneo (and elsewhere), bearded pigs have the greatest ecological impact of any species apart from humans. As they disrupt the forest floor, a wide range of other species take advantage. Ground-dwelling birds such as pheasants, partridges and the rarely-seen endemic, Bornean ground-cuckoo, may spend long period at these wallows, picking up exposed invertebrates and seeds.

The pigs' biggest influence, however, is on the structure of the rainforest itself. Their activities influence the distribution of many rainforest tree species, especially the predominant family known as dipterocarps, as well as oak acorns and chestnut. Bearded pigs are addicted to the oil-rich seeds of these trees and often consume all of the seeds available in an area. In the short term, this means there is no germination for the trees and little high-quality food for the pigs. When the seeds have all been eaten, they resort to anything edible: worms, seedlings, ferns and even grass. But high intakes of the oily seeds are required by the females for breeding. This means that reproduction in both trees and pigs is on hold until there are more seeds.

The trees have developed an effective solution to this problem, something honed over millions of years. At irregular intervals – between four to eleven years – all of the trees in a particular area produce colossal amounts of seeds, a phenomenon known as 'masting'. This evolutionary strategy 'floods the market' with so much product that it would be impossible for all the seeds to be consumed. These mass flowering and fruiting events often involve numerous species of trees somehow coordinating their reproductive efforts over a few months. How they accomplish this is not known, but the ecological impact is enormous. During these events, the forest is spectacularly transformed, with swirling clouds of winged seeds spiralling down from the canopy resembling what has been called a 'tropical blizzard'. Vast amounts of seeds accumulate in 'snow drifts' around fallen trunks and stumps. And the entire ecosystem responds!

These periodic booms of massive amounts of high-quality food drive the reproduction cycles of a diverse array of forest creatures: wasps and moths, pigeons and porcupines, pheasants, civets, and many others. The snowstorms of seeds fuel an ecosystem-wide orgy (well, yes …) of breeding that will shape entire populations for years to come. And none more so than the pigs.

These spectacular masting events are not evenly spread over the landscape. Some areas will be knee-deep in seeds while others may have more modest harvests, or none at all. Tracking the flowering patterns over large areas is extremely difficult for ecologists even today, despite the latest technology. Yet the pigs seem to know just when and where they must go to find the best foraging locations. Moving in search of the seed bonanzas is the driving force behind their mass migrations. It's crucial to get the time and place right: they need to anticipate the flowering of the trees so that the females are pregnant when masting is underway. Gorging on the seeds provides the nutrients required by their suckling piglets. During a masting year, and if they can find the right places, a female can produce a second litter of up to a dozen young within six months.

On extremely rare occasions, up to forty species of tree will mast sequentially and in adjacent valleys, prolonging the boom times, sometimes for several years. Such events can lead to spectacular population growth among the pigs. This was the most likely explanation for the gigantic herd witnessed by Gurong. These events have occurred in Borneo for millennia – creating the largest biomass of any animal species on the island – and have literally shaped the rainforests themselves.


THESE ORDINARY (IF UNTIDY) LOOKING PIGS ALSO have an enormous influence on the people who live on the island. Bearded pigs have been the primary source of protein for most of Borneo's original human inhabitants for at least 40000 years. This changed with the arrival of the pork-averse Muslims in the tenth century, but their influence was confined primarily to coastal areas. Even ten years ago, bearded pig meat still accounted for almost 40 per cent of all the meat consumed by inland communities. Hunting bearded pigs remains an integral part of the lives of most of the indigenous people of Borneo.

This relationship between the trees, the pigs and the original people is as deeply intertwined as any human–nature interaction on the planet. And it has shaped the lives and beliefs of the indigenous people of Borneo in profound ways. Such a complex ecological and cultural connection relies on the continuation of ages-old patterns of behaviour and movement. And none more so than the mass migrations of bearded pigs, setting out during a masting year in search of the next best source of oil-rich seeds. The mountainous topography of Borneo means that some migration routes funnel the travelling herds into places such as narrow river crossings, where they can be more easily hunted. Traditionally, spears were used, although all hunters also have rifles these days. Only enough animals are killed as can be transported back to the village; there is little point in taking too many. These logistical constraints resulted in genuine sustainable harvesting practices that have ensured the continuation of the entire complex relationship.

It would be impossible to overemphasise the significant of bearded pigs to the indigenous people of Borneo. When I asked Gurong what his job was, his answer was pragmatic: 'I am pig hunter. Hunting is what I am.' And yet, this very identity is now under serious threat as the fundamentals of the migration become harder and harder to maintain. This is not because of the native trees – masting still happens –

and it's not due to overhunting. The main issue has been the replacement of an entire impossibly complex tropical rainforest ecosystem with a single tree species, oil palm, over enormous areas of Borneo.

Oil palm. An ordinary looking palm with a broad trunk and dense, spiky fronds that produce lots of ordinary-looking bunches of fruit which look, when fully ripe, like maroon, chicken-egg–sized rugby balls. Squeeze them hard enough and a rich yellow fluid dribbles out: palm oil. This liquid is the most important edible oil on the planet, far more valuable than its main rivals, canola and sunflower. It is the most productive of the edible oils, meaning many more litres of oil per area than for any of the other oil-producing crops. It is also extremely efficient in terms of the work required to grow the crop. Canola and sunflower are annuals, lasting only a single year, so have to be planted again annually. Oil palm trees can be harvested at about three years of age and continue to produce for another twenty. Palm oil is now used in about 40 per cent of all products found on a typical supermarket shelf. These include cosmetics, soap, detergents, and an astounding number of processed food products such as ice cream, chocolate and breads.

There are, however, two big problems with oil palms. First, the trees grow best in tropical lowlands, in environments and climates similar to that of their original distribution in tropical West Africa. These hot, humid equatorial areas are also the world's most biodiverse ecosystems: tropical rainforests. The Amazon, West Africa and Borneo used to have the largest expanses of these forests, but all have lost major areas to oil palm plantations.

The expansion of oil palm plantations throughout Borneo has been rapid and extensive. During the 1960s, timber was the main source of income, the island exporting more tropical timber than anywhere else in the world. The whole-scale removal of rainforest for wood was perfect timing for the burgeoning palm oil industry. The recently cleared areas were quickly planted with oil palm seedlings. By the 1980s, less than twenty years later, palm oil had become Sabah's most important source of income. The area under cultivation of this single tree species reached almost two million hectares and covered 24 per cent of Sabah's total land area.

The growth of Sabah's oil palm industry has slowed in recent times, due simply to the lack of suitable land. Virtually everywhere that could grow the trees is now full. In addition, new environmental protection laws (belatedly) banning the clearing of any primary rainforest within the state have played a part. This enlightened legislation is very welcome, but long overdue. The damage has been done and cannot be reversed; once an area has had two rotations of planting, a period spanning about sixty years, the soil is virtually useless for commercial purposes. Typically, such areas are abandoned, and quickly become covered in dense, weedy regrowth. These areas are classed as 'secondary forest', but the resemblance to primary rainforest is minimal. These dense and scrappy areas are not useful to bearded pigs or to the people that hunt them.

The vast expanses of the distinctively sharp and shiny deep-green oil palms are impossible to miss in Borneo. During our day-long road trip from Kota Kinabalu to

Maliau Basin, the view is of endless, monotonous fern-encrusted tree trunks with virtually no understorey. The solid canopy of palm fronds shades the space beneath in a subterranean gloom. It could hardly be more different to the complexity and diversity of the tropical rainforest it has replaced. The reduction of biodiversity that results from this transition is, not unexpectedly, extreme. Not many animals are able to use this new and shockingly simplified habitat. But, ironically, bearded pigs do.

Something that bearded pigs find irresistible are oil-rich seeds and the floors of palm plantations, at certain times of the year, are liberally sprinkled with the small juicy orbs that contain them. This new food source has had several implications for the pigs. At the starkest end, the replacement of tropical forest with this monoculture over such an enormous geographic scale has dramatically disrupted their traditional migration activities and routes. The animals are unable to find their way through the mosaic of cleared land and plantations; most traditional landmarks have been obliterated.

There is also evidence that the fragmentation of the landscape by the plantations has affected the masting behaviour of the native trees, although no one is clear about why. This may mean that the millennia-long ecological relationships between the rainforest trees and the pigs have been profoundly disrupted: the trees are masting less often, and the pigs can't find their way through the new unfamiliar landscape.

They may not be moving through the plantations, but they are visiting them to consume the fallen fruit.

While there, they do what all pigs do: root around in the soil and consume whatever they consider edible. This includes plenty of palm seedlings, a practice that has turned them into destructive pests in the eyes of the plantation managers.

The identity of most of the indigenous people of the interior of Sabah (and, indeed, Borneo as a whole) has been thoroughly intertwined with the hunting of bearded pigs. This relationship has developed over thousands of years and is deeply embedded in the cultural and religious fabric of the numerous communities still living at least partial traditional lives. Anything that disrupted this close connection would have incredibly serious consequences for the indigenous people. The arrival of oil palm has done exactly that. Ancient customs and cultural practices have been severely altered. Bearded pig meat is much more than the most important source of protein throughout the island for millennia – the meat is a critical element in religious and social ceremonies, and an important form of gift-giving. Hunting pigs has been the primary activity of the able-bodied males since 'the beginning', conferring status and prestige. All of these customs and cultural norms have been utterly transformed by the arrival of oil palms.

Within a horrifyingly short time, the numbers of pigs and their distribution have changed. Hunters must travel much further to find them, and there are fewer to kill. The movements of the pigs appear to be more localised, and their migrations have diminished markedly in scale and regularity. This is especially evident close to the plantations. Smaller movements mean that the animals are remaining for longer in the same location, isolated populations that are soon hunted out. In many villages, the supply of pig meat is no longer reliable. Formerly legendary and revered pig hunters have had to leave the forest and seek paid employment for the first time in their people's history. This has been profoundly distressing and disorientating for a proud people defined by pig hunting. To add to this already unsettling scenario, their skills as hunters are now deployed not in the testing of prowess through the worthy pursuit of bearded pigs deep in the forest, but in 'controlling pests'. Today, about a quarter of indigenous people in Sabah work at some time for the plantations.

WHEN I MET GURONG IN JULY 2019, HE WAS PENSIVE but remained cautiously optimistic about the future. Little did we both realise that the entire world was about to change dramatically. Covid was about to strike and cancel everything. For me, it would be my last trip to Maliau, the eighth in a row. For Gurong and the indigenous pig hunters of Borneo, it was much more than an inconvenience. Even far from the towns, movement of people was severely restricted, making hunting expeditions even harder. Things for these people were about to go from bad to catastrophic.

In December 2020, the first dead bearded pig was noticed, near the Kinabatangan River in eastern Sabah. Finding an intact dead pig was unusual; if they had been killed by a predator, there would be nothing left. When about twenty others were found over the next few weeks, it was clear that something was not right. The vets confirmed their worst fears: African swine flu had arrived in Borneo. This was almost inevitable; the disease has been spreading through the Philippines and peninsular Malaysia in recent months, and so was expected. Still, hearing about it from afar and experiencing it yourself are very different things.

This disease is both deadly and extremely contagious. For gregarious animals like bearded pigs, its impact is swift and dramatic. And arriving in the midst of the Covid lockdowns seemed horribly unfortunate. With travel anywhere severely restricted for months, monitoring the passage of the disease through the island, which would have been difficult anyway, became virtually impossible.

By the time travel restrictions were lifted, assessments of the number of pigs killed by the virus were indeed shocking. Outbreaks were confirmed in twenty of the twenty-three districts of Sabah, with most recording losses of 90 per cent of the original populations. When the hunters were finally able to visit their main hunting sites, they found them eerily quiet: no muffled grunting, no little squeals of piglet disputes, no occasional belches from the old males.

Unfortunately, the bearded pigs at Maliau did not survive the epidemic. When the staff returned to the station after the Covid lockdowns, they found the Boss dead near his usual scavenging location. No other individuals were seen, and they had not returned at the time of writing (March 2025).

The forests have lost their gardeners and the people, their connection to an entire way of life. Borneo has been changed forever.

# (4)
## ELEPHANT MEMORIES

ONE'S FIRST DAWN AT MALIAU BASIN IS ALWAYS special. You wake very early, eager to start the day. It's not completely dark and not completely quiet. Faint light from the still-starry sky illuminates the rectangular shape of the window in my room, but outside is in deep shadow. The vertical wall of dense rainforest, only a few metres away, seems to absorb the light, postponing the visual until later. Instead, it's all auditory. A mosaic of sounds: small, delicate trills, chirps, twittering, morse code pops and ticks, tiny, filigreed patterns of insect, frog and gecko voices. Together, they weave an intricate tapestry of interconnected sounds, a sparkling sonic shawl. It's a soothing and gentle transition into the new day.

As the sky lightens, louder, less calming sounds slowly rise in volume: screeching, chattering, bugling and shouting as myriad birds and mammals advertise their presence. There are lots of calls, but I'm waiting for something specific: one of the defining sounds of this place.

Here they go!

OOOOOOO, oo, oo, oo …

Oh, oh, OOOOOO, ooooooo …

AHHH, AHHH!

Gibbons! A glorious, outrageous, vibrant broadcast of whoops, whoos and hollow wailing, punctuated by high-intensity screams and sneers. As a statement of territorial occupation, robust wellbeing and uncompromising presence, this morning chorus is hard to beat. It's still too dark to see them, high up in the canopy, but they are very close this morning. The strident howling usually only lasts for a few minutes, but if another troop is nearby and is willing to challenge, the vocal combat can carry on well into the morning. Most of the adults in the troop contribute to the ear-bursting cacophony; it's impossible not to feel wide awake with that welcome to the morning!

Breakfast is always at 7 am and dinner at 7 pm, so our days revolve around these markers. This allows a good hour between first light (in the tropics, dawn is abrupt) and eating, so there's time for some exploration. Last year, a young sun bear was discovered, asleep in a hollow log, its snout still sticky from gorging on a huge honeycomb. Yesterday, I saw a massive great slaty woodpecker – the world's largest – hammering loudly high up in a dead tree. And it pays to be attentive; I almost put my hand on a small viper which matched the vivid green of the leaves it was coiled within.

These are rare but memorable encounters. But some equally exciting moments happen on most days. You never fail to stop and watch a pair of pterodactyl-sized helmeted hornbills, flying only a few metres above head height, their loud, ponderous wingbeats – seemingly too slow to keep such a huge bird in the air – sounding like 'the breaths a sleeping volcano would make', as one student memorably described it.

I am with a group of undergraduate students from Australia, staying at the Maliau Basin Study Centre. The students are participating in a tropical ecology course and, on this first morning, everyone is still naïvely enthusiastic. The humidity, mud and leeches will moderate the mood over the two weeks, but for the moment, the wonder all around us is energising.

After breakfast on the first morning, we assemble at one of the laboratories for the standard safety briefing, to hear about the station's rules and meet the guides who are going to work with us each day. These people are professional research assistants, knowledgeable guides and general minders. They have been thoroughly trained and are experienced in a wide variety of skills, including emergency medical treatment. Quite simply, our activities would be impossible without them.

All excursions into the forest are only allowed in groups, and must not be very far from the station. For longer excursions, it is critical to be accompanied by one or more guides. Although these people are employed to assist with logistics in the field and share their ecological knowledge, one of their most important roles lies in elephant detection. While we are preoccupied with chasing butterflies or watching birds through binoculars, the guides unobtrusively scan for any signs of elephant presence. A pile of dung is an obvious sign, but they will also be looking for trampled grass, footprints in the leaf litter, hints of their musky scent, or the low-pitched rumbling sound they make when communicating at close quarters. If any of these signs are detected, there is no argument: everyone has to stop whatever they are doing, gather their things and retreat. If the dung is very fresh or rumbling is detected, it means 'LEAVE NOW! IMMEDIATELY! GO!'

I initially felt this elephant paranoia to be exaggerated. I had seen and interacted with Asian elephants in parks in Thailand, and my general impression was of cheerful gentle giants, kids on their backs, being fed sugarcane by tourists. The most violent thing I had seen them do was playfully spray some visitors with a trunk-full of river water. But that impression – based on healthy captive animals, well-trained and thoroughly used to people – could not be applied to free-ranging (feral, even) elephants living away from humans in the rainforests of Borneo.

Although the origins of these elephants – technically known as Bornean pygmy elephants, a distinct race of the Asian elephant – is still contested, the ancestors of the current population were present on the island around 300 000 years ago. Small numbers have been sent and exchanged over the years with other nations, but little is known of what became of them. And it doesn't explain why Bornean elephants are so malicious.

Some have suggested that the most badly behaved animals are descended from those recruited (enslaved?) as beasts of burden. Certainly, many were treated appallingly. While some were used for ceremonial purposes, carrying the nobility or army generals around, seated on huge platforms, most were condemned much more menial tasks:

dragging enormous logs to sawmills, and other hard work. They were frequently abused, beaten, and trained in macabre and painful ways. 'It's no mystery why the elephants are so aggressive,' explained one of the station's staff when the risks of elephant encounters were being discussed. 'They were hurt by people and have never forgotten. They remember and tell their children. They tell them how badly they were treated and now, decades later, new generations still hate us. The mahouts [trainers] were often cruel. You can't blame the elephants. They were abused a lot!'

Whether they actually hate us is beside the point; every year, people are chased and trampled, houses destroyed, crops uprooted and cars wrecked. The elephants seem especially triggered by people on foot. Just before our arrival in 2017, a tourist was crushed to death when she approached a herd beside the road, not far from the Maliau Basin entrance gate. She was trying to take a selfie. Being near these animals is genuinely risky, and sometimes deadly. Which is why we depend on the guides to be vigilant.

But sometimes you (that is, I) might make a poor decision.

We had arrived at the station very late the day before. The safety briefing had been delayed because the guides had not yet turned up, so we had some time on our hands. A small group of students were particularly enthusiastic and impatient and wanted to head off immediately to explore. You could hardly blame them. The previous day had been spent crammed inside a hot, noisy minibus and now they had finally arrived at the place they had been dreaming about for months. In every direction, tropical jungle spread into the misty distance.

What were we waiting for? Let's go!

Ignoring the safety protocols, I decided to take them to the conjunction of two rivers outside the Basin, about a forty-minute walk. Yes, it would be without a guide, but hey! I knew the spiel and had watched how the guides did it. Everything would be fine.

Although I tried to keep noise to a minimum, everyone was animated by excitement. Literally everything was new and amazing. The track passed through a section of forest that had been harvested for the timber used to build the station. The rainforest had grown back vigorously in the twenty years since. Regenerating areas like this are known as secondary forest and feature an almost impenetrable layer of dense understorey and small trees. Primary rainforest, such as occurs inside the Basin itself, is darker, dominated by enormous trees, with a lot less understorey. Above the dense understorey, secondary forest was more open, making it far easier to detect birds. And there were plenty. Every few minutes something different would land on a branch or careen through the air just above our heads. A spectacular greater racket-tailed drongo appeared suddenly on an exposed limb, looking agitated and spitting out strange electronic sounds. These glossy black, hyperactive birds seem always on edge, their twin tail plumes twitching with electric energy. Somewhere through the trees, the unmistakable rapid-fire drumming of a woodpecker began.

For these young ecologists, it could hardly have been

more exciting. As we progressed slowly down the track, the forest began to close in around us. Only very light logging had occurred this far in – only a few specific trees had been felled – and the forest was almost fully intact. Along the edges of the track, however, the understorey was thick and impenetrable. It became darker and quieter as the canopy closed above us. It became harder to see far, and the trees were taller.

We became aware of the sound of rushing water nearby. Through a gap in the vegetation we could see the light glittering off the waters of the Maliau River, every drop of which had originated as rain inside the Basin. We were getting close to the end of the track. It finished at a narrow triangle of land where the two rivers – the Maliau and the Kuamut – meet. A dead end. I was pointing this out to the students, explaining that the only way out was back the way we had come when the relative quiet was punctured by a shockingly loud bugle-like trumpeting.

We all stopped dead.

'Was that –?' someone asked.

We looked through the gloom in the direction of the noise. It was fairly dark but there was no doubt: the unmistakable shape of a raised elephant truck.

SHIT!

This was serious. There were elephants near us.

When I looked again, the trunk had disappeared.

Everyone was alert. Silent. Listening hard. And they were all looking at me.

I needed to take charge; to appear calm, and not panic.

'Yes. There are elephants. It's okay. They seem to have gone away. But we need to leave. Now!'

Most people began walking briskly, occasionally glancing back. Then I noticed that a couple of stragglers had just arrived, and were not sure what was going on.

'What? Elephants? Really? Cool. Where were they?'

I turned and gestured frantically for them to start walking. 'Definitely elephants, but they can be dangerous. They're not that close, but we can't be sure. We have to go now!'

As if to prove the point, the dense understorey and saplings on the edge of the forest only 20 metres away began to sway violently. Very loud trumpeting – undeniably threatening – blasted from the other side of the blustering foliage.

The two students' expressions changed instantly from carefree fascination to barely contained terror. They looked at me: *What do we do?*

What did the guides say? I'd heard it a dozen times. Something about walking quickly away in the opposite direction. But not to run, as you could trip.

'Go. Fast! But walk, don't run.'

And another fact came to mind: elephants can run much faster than us. You can't outrun them, even in the jungle. And they can move quickly without making noise.

I looked ahead. Some of the students had stopped, uncertain, waiting for me.

In a low but clear voice, I said, 'Keep going. To the bridge. Don't run, but don't stop.'

Our pace was now fast and steady. Everyone was

striding ahead, focused on the ground directly in front of them, making sure they didn't trip. The only sounds we could hear were our footsteps and rapid breathing. In about ten minutes we had covered quite a distance. There had been no more terrifying sounds from the forest. Surely we were safe now.

At that precise moment, the vegetation immediately to our left began to thrash violently. Had they been stalking us this whole time, making no noise at all? It seemed impossible. But there it was again: trumpeting, deafening, much closer this time.

We had to make it over the small bridge to be safe. The elephants would not cross it and the banks of the stream it spans are too steep for them. But they had almost cut us off. Panic began to spread. Some of the students were close to tears. A number of them bolted, making a run for it. One immediately slipped, sprawling face-first into the mud. Two of her friends pulled her up and they strode ahead.

We rounded a corner and saw the bridge at last, down a slippery slope of deep muddy track. The fastest students had already crossed over. I allowed myself a tiny amount of relief.

But again, this was shattered by the blaring of elephants and the violent movement of the understorey vegetation, very close this time.

'The bridge! Quick!' I shouted. The students gingerly moved down the slope, going as quickly as they could. It looked like they were all going to make it, but I had to be sure. I stopped and faced the forest in the direction of the swaying foliage. It was only about 5 metres away this time. Another of the guide's instructions popped into my head: 'If they charge, move behind a tree.'

I glanced around. There were plenty of trees, but the understorey was impenetrable. There was no way I'd be able to get behind a tree.

Before I had the chance to think of an alternative, with a deafening blare a huge male burst through the understorey that had so successfully kept him hidden. Somewhere in my mind I noted that this was the first time I had actually seen one close-up. Every feature of his immense body seemed hardened with power and determination. I didn't stand a chance.

Then he stopped. I could smell his odour, hot and musky. His little eyes were bright with agitation.

He raised his trunk and trumpeted again, a tremendous blast. And then, as I watched, frozen, he seemed to vanish, backing away, disappearing into the green shadowy gloom.

I stayed rooted to the spot. Staring into the forest. Pulse racing, blood pounding in my temples.

I don't know how long I stood there. Eventually, I remembered to breathe. I turned to walk, and nearly fell over. I was still trembling violently. But I was alive.

So were the students. They had been watching from the other side of the bridge. When I looked up, their faces were ashen, eyes wide and alarmed. A few hands reached out to pat my back and shoulders, but the reactions and words could wait. For now, we simply needed to be as far away from here as possible.

Over the following days, I spent time revisiting what

had happened. I had made a critical error of judgment. It could have ended very differently. I also checked on the students. As far as I could tell, they saw it as a brilliant adventure story to tell their friends.

ONLY SIX MONTHS LATER I HAD A VERY DIFFERENT encounter with Asian elephants. I had travelled to Chiang Mai in northern Thailand to meet a student, Emily Flower, who was investigating the treatment of captive elephants in a range of tourist parks. Chiang Mai is the epicentre of elephant-based tourism in South-East Asia, with most of Thailand's famous elephant parks located in this vicinity. Interacting with these enormous beasts in one of the main drawcards of the country; of the many millions of tourists who visit Thailand annually, about 70 per cent say that seeing elephants is a key objective. And there are many venues to choose from – two hundred and fifty in total! Where you go depends on what you want in the way of interaction: riding up high on a wooden platform like a sultan going out to battle, seeing them perform circus tricks such as walking on their back legs, watching them play soccer, or taking home a unique painting produced by an elephant just for you.

It's hard to reconcile the sight of a gigantic and regal animal smearing paint on a canvas with the laborious activities of only a few decades earlier. While elephants have been a central part of military, ceremonial and cultural life in Thailand for centuries, more recently most were engaged in the timber industry. All captive elephants are under the direct control of mahouts, the traditional handlers, who train and manage every aspect of their animal's lives. Young elephants undergo years of 'breaking in' to ensure they are safe to be around people and that they will obey the directions of their handlers. This is an absolute necessity for such a big powerful animal, something I didn't need convincing of.

Mahouts and their elephants had been an integral component of the logging industry in Thailand, mainly as beasts of burden that hauled massive logs to the timber mills and transport hubs. They were especially useful in difficult terrain that the timber jigs (log trucks) could not reach. It was tough and exhausting work, but it provided a steady income for a mahout and his family. For the elephants, it was a life of relentless hardship and frequent pain; they were often beaten and jabbed to keep them compliant.

That all changed almost instantly in 1989. A series of catastrophic landslips and mudslides following prolonged rains were – correctly – attributed to the wholescale clearing of the forest from vast areas in central Thailand. The government's kneejerk response was to immediately ban all logging. The huge and profitable timber industry ceased to exist overnight. Large numbers of people who had worked in the industry for generations suddenly found themselves looking for alternative employment, not an easy situation in the remote areas of the country. Many had no choice but to move to the big cities in search of work.

The impact of the logging ban was particularly serious

for the handlers and their families, and of course, their elephants. A fundamental issue was how to feed an animal that requires about 250 kilograms of plant material every day. Many mahouts were reduced to begging in the streets, a demeaning and dangerous activity.

The arrival of elephants and their handers in an established tourist destination such as Chiang Mai, however, offered an obvious opportunity for attracting paying visitors. Starting in the early 1990s, the number of venues featuring elephants began to proliferate. Many operators had no experience with elephants, but they did have a good idea what tourists would pay to see. The emphasis was on entertainment, the more exotic and bizarre the better. Being well trained and compliant, the elephants did what they were told, regardless of how degrading and ridiculous the activity. I was shocked to hear of elephants being forced to dance and walk on their hind legs, something exceedingly dangerous and entirely unnatural. The mahouts had to train their charges to carry out very different tasks to what had been required out in the jungle. Traditional training methods were almost all based on painful jabs and prods using the standard tool of all mahouts, the 'hook'. This apparatus comes in a variety of designs, but all feature a sharp point that can be applied to sensitive parts of the elephant's anatomy. During the early years of the burgeoning elephant tourism industry, very little attention was paid to how the animals were treated. As long as the visitors handed over their cash and left without complaint, there was little motivation to do things differently. Some places were exemplary in their treatment of the animals. Many were appalling. This was of little consequence for many years.

However, things began to change when the welfare of any animals under the care of people became a topic of great interest worldwide. The treatment of animals in zoos and circuses, in particular, came in for severe criticism, and most altered their practices drastically. They had to: the audiences were voting with their feet.

The elephant parks were no exception to this scrutiny. Many tourists didn't hesitate to share their thoughts on social media. Reviews and ratings on websites such as Tripadvisor have become an essential component of selecting places to visit. Prospective visitors could read the candid reviews from any number of hypersensitive attendees. The problem was, most of the people writing these comments were not trained or experienced in their evaluations. They may have been reacting to something entirely routine, or missing something else that was of far greater consequence. What would be really useful was a simple but comprehensive tool that anyone could use to assess a venue. This had to be based on the latest research, yet easy to use. Such an approach would provide a reliable way to evaluate and compare elephant venues.

Emily Flower was undertaking a PhD on the treatment of elephants in Thailand. As a tourist herself a few years previously, she had seen firsthand how some places treated their animals. She was determined to come up with irrefutable evidence of poor practices, so that visitors could make informed decisions about which places to support. She developed the Rapid Elephant Welfare

Assessment Method (or REWAM), a comprehensive tool that was relatively easy to administer. But it still needed to be tested in the field. Or, more appropriately, in the elephant parks; that's why we were here.

I was waiting for Emily in the hotel lobby. My recent encounter with the Bornean elephants was seared into my brain, but the elephants we would be seeing today were used to people and apparently enjoyed their work. At least that's what the Nirvana Elephant Sanctuary website (not its real name) boldly stated. It also claimed that hooks were not used and visitors would spend the day 'communing with these gentle giants' in an 'entirely natural setting'. I thought it sounded pretty good.

Emily was less convinced. 'Yeah, well, all this proves is that the operators know what to say to placate your average Western tourist. I've heard it all before. It's what actually happens that's more important. Let's see how Nirvana shapes up.'

Our journey to Nirvana in a minibus took almost an hour. The roads became progressively steeper and windier and the jungle denser as we travelled. As we disembarked at the entrance to the sanctuary, one of the staff stepped forward and asked for our attention. We were told that the purpose of this facility was focused primarily on the welfare of the elephants; entertaining visitors was not the priority. All of the interaction we would have had been designed to facilitate their recovery and rehabilitation.

'There won't be any silly antics or party tricks. Some of these animals carry deep psychological scars from neglect and abuse; all have experienced some level of trauma.

They are patients, not performers, although none of the elephants you will meet today are in any way dangerous. We assume that you have come all this way because you support what we are doing. If this isn't what you had hoped for, we will be happy to refund you in full.'

I was impressed. Emily looked indifferent.

We were led down a steep path to a broad flat area and asked to wait for the arrival of the elephants. They soon appeared from a narrow opening in the jungle, almost sprinting into the open, looking eager and alert, their mahouts close by. But it wasn't us they were interested in – it was the piles of sugarcane pieces that had been dumped on the ground behind us. I looked up to see Emily taking notes already.

'Too many sweet snacks,' she mouthed noiselessly. Not a good start, apparently.

Each of us was assigned an elephant which we were to accompany throughout the visit. When 'my' companion rushed towards me, vivid memories of the Borneo encounter flashed before me. I stood very stiffly as Rajah, a massive mature male, brushed past, trying to keep my impulse to run under control. But he was soon delicately picking up pieces of sugarcane with his trunk and inserting them into his mouth, munching contentedly. When I still hadn't moved, he lifted a large piece and presented it to me with his trunk, as if to say, 'Well, come on! Don't you know you're supposed to be feeding me this stuff?'

Emily was already applying her REWAM assessment, although you would have to have been watching carefully to know. Her objective was to assess a number of venues, hopefully representing a decent sample of the hundreds of elephant facilities in the country. It was important to cover the full range of the quality available, from the appalling to the exemplary. From the website blurb and the statement made by the head guide, one might think that Nirvana would be one of the better operations, but we would see. This was a road test of the assessment technique, to ensure it was reliable and easy to use. Emily had assessed four venues so far, and told me she was fairly pleased with how it was going.

'The hardest part is pretending you're just another tourist enjoying the experience while surreptitiously taking notes,' Emily had explained before we arrived. 'The venue operators and owners have approved this assessment, and they'll all receive detailed feedback, but I have to be very discreet. If the mahouts know they're being evaluated, they'd probably act very differently.'

The REWAM was designed to cover a wide variety of parameters, in an attempt to include everything that contributed – negatively or positively – to the welfare of the elephants. Some were associated with the venue's physical features: the substrate the animals walked on, the types of shelters, the size of the enclosures. Others covered features of the animals themselves: their behaviour and social interactions, as well as a Body Condition Score. This well-established method developed for evaluating elephants living in zoos focuses on the build and general appearance of the animal. Emily had undergone training in Australia in order to be able to perform this important measure properly. Finally, some parameters relating to the interactions between the mahouts and their charges were included. This required careful but clandestine observations of the handlers as they went about their normal activities.

It wasn't long before Emily silently caught my attention and indicated with a subtly raised chin a mahout and elephant walking past. I glanced at the pair and couldn't see anything unusual. When I looked back to Emily she mouthed 'Hook.' The mahout now had his back to us and I noticed that he was indeed carrying something in his right hand. He was attempting to keep it out of sight, but the sharp metal point was clearly visible.

Simply carrying the hook – the basic instrument used in training elephants – didn't necessarily mean that it was being used. But this discovery – and the fact that it was obviously being kept out of sight – made us alert to any other features being hidden from the view of visitors.

After finishing the piles of sugarcane, it was time for a wash. Each elephant and their visitor followed its mahout down to the river, a slowly flowing stream with gently sloping edges. The animals flopped over onto their sides in the shallows and waited while we scrubbed their back and legs with a coarse brush. The whole time they made strange deep booming noises, so deep and low that it was hard to know where they were coming from. They were never entirely quiet (though I was thankful that at no stage did they give a trumpeting blast!).

While the elephants – who seemed to be on good terms with each other – relaxed in the water, Emily gave me a whispered summary of her evaluations so far.

'Nirvana may not quite be elephant paradise, but it's

scoring pretty well,' she said quietly, after making certain no one else was within earshot. 'The fact that the animals are allowed to socialise freely and actively encouraged to practise natural behaviours, like what they're doing now' – this included playfully squirting water at each other – 'and that they get to walk on natural ground rather than concrete floors are all good signs. I'll be interested to know what health checks they receive and where they're kept when there aren't any visitors around.'

The head mahout (the one with the concealed weapon) now shouted that it was time for 'riding'. That was a surprise. Most of what I had read suggested that riding wasn't regarded favourably by most of the venues that sold themselves as humane and up-to-date. Emily had her poker face on, but I knew she was taking notes mentally.

We all wandered back to the assembly area, where the head guide explained what was to happen. He said that the riding was strictly bareback and that taking part was always optional (for the humans, presumably; I don't think the elephants got a say). He said that the riding was only for about twenty minutes, was all on dirt tracks through the jungle, and was an important part of the enrichment program that provided both exercise and mental stimulation. 'So if you would like to mount your noble steeds, the mahouts have them ready for you.'

Around us the eight elephants were all kneeling with one of the front legs forming a kind of step. Riders were able to climb onto the animal's back and swing their legs over so that they sat on the neck, their legs hidden behind the enormous ears.

I was unsure about whether I should be so closely involved with the animals. I looked over to Emily for guidance. 'Ride if you like. One person riding bareback isn't too bad for the elephant. And it would be good to see what it's like here, especially if it's regarded as beneficial in terms of behavioural enrichment. This is the first time I've heard it described that way,' she said. I was a little surprised.

'I won't ride,' she said. 'I've done it in the past and am not entirely comfortable with it. But more importantly, I want to do some more observations and this is a perfect opportunity.'

I hoisted myself up onto Rajah's neck while Emily fell to the back of the procession; it looked as though she was doing more Body Condition Scores. Only one other person had declined the riding option; six of the eight elephants made up the trekking group.

The mahouts walked off to the side of the single-file group, chatting and laughing. The elephants obviously knew where they were going and didn't need to be led. My ride, Rajah, was the largest of all and quickly moved to the front, setting a brisk pace until we were well ahead of the rest. We lost sight of the others when we turned a corner and he seemed to relax, or that's how I interpreted his mood. He flapped his ears, shook his head and gave a small trumpet, as though ridding himself of a bit of stress. He moved off the track slightly to pluck a substantial trunkful of long green grass which he chewed messily for the rest of the trek.

After an uneventful walk we arrived at a series of

buildings and enclosures. This was the headquarters of the operation, where the animals spent most of their days when not engaged with visitors. Rajah stopped abruptly outside a large gate and ponderously knelt in the same stance as before. I dismounted and he immediately moved through the gate into a large arena. As the others dawdled in, each made the same movement until all riders had been safely accounted for. This arena wasn't accessible to the public, but we could see what was happening behind the fence. Each elephant had moved to a specific location where a huge dish of leaves, fruit and grass was waiting for them. As they began to feed, the mahouts quietly attached a collar and chain to one of their hind legs. This was unexpected, to me at least.

One of the staff was wandering past, carrying a wicker broom. He greeted me with a broad smile so I called him over. 'How long are the elephants chained?' I asked, trying to appear simply curious. 'Until next visitors come. Today, one hour. Yesterday, no visitors, so chained all day.' He beamed his smile again and wandered off, presumably feeling pleased that he had been able to engage with the tourists.

We had reached the end of the tour. It had been a fascinating day and there was plenty of animated banter among the small group of visitors as we waited for the minibus to arrive. A middle-aged American couple were particularly effusive. 'Wasn't that marvellous,' the woman gushed. 'What happy elephants! What wonderful handlers! It's almost perfect, isn't it! I'll be giving it the highest possible rating on Tripadvisor.'

I caught Emily's eye. 'So would you agree,' I asked very quietly. 'Perfect?'

Scanning to ensure no one else could hear, she said, 'No, a long way from perfect. But in the scheme of things, this place is not too bad. It was doing pretty well in terms of ratings – the conditions here are excellent, the mahouts are well trained and clearly know what they're doing. They do daily foot checks and the enrichment activities are all great. The Body Scores were all fine, although the amount of sugary treats is probably excessive. Sugarcane is okay in moderate quantities, but the amount they get daily could have health risks. I wonder how often they check their teeth.'

Emily paused to look over at the now immobile row of animals. The two closest were straining on their chains and reaching out to each other with their trucks, but were several metres too short.

'Look at that,' she said quietly. 'They've deliberately positioned them so they can't touch. Why would they do that? That's going to reduce the rating a bit more. And then there's the hook. It isn't always a bad thing, but it depends how it's used.'

'Excuse me.' A mahout had suddenly materialised next to us. Emily and I exchanged a quick glance. (Had he heard anything?) If so, he didn't show it. But what he said was a surprise.

He swept his arm from behind his back to reveal a large wooden handle with an arc of pointed metal: the infamous mahout's hook. We then realised that this was the handler Emily had noticed trying to conceal it. Yet, here he was displaying it openly before us. The three of us were standing well away from the other visitors; none of them were looking at us.

'I have been watching you,' he said matter-of-factly. 'When you noticed my hook earlier, I thought that you may be worried about it. Please, let me explain. I am the head mahout and I am the only one authorised to carry a hook. You see, all of these animals know what the hook is for. Pain. Yes, pain. They were all trained by using hooks and it still has power over them. However, we very rarely use it like that anymore. But because the elephants know it, it is very important if we ever need to control their behaviour. It is for the safety of the visitors and the other elephants. I don't want to tell you how to rate us, but this is why I – and only I – carry the hook. My job is to watch all the elephants carefully. I also notice things about our visitors.' He smiled knowingly and walked away.

It has been several years since Emily completed her research. While she has published many of her findings in the scientific journals, it is in social media where the strongest impact has been felt. Visitors have responded quickly to her descriptions of elephant treatment. Most importantly, reviews on travel websites have been extremely influential on tourist choices. Many elephant parks now actively promote their welfare concerns and claim they have changed their ways. It's impossible to verify whether this is due to Emily's important work, but it will certainly have played a part in the general change in perception of elephants in captivity.

# (5)

## CROSSING the ROAD

WE CAN'T SEE THE ROAD, BUT IT'S CLOSE, SOME-where beyond the dense wall of vegetation we are heading towards. There's the deep, pulsating, dull roar of constant traffic punctuated occasionally by the higher-pitched whine of a motorcycle. Despite the thick screen of shrubs and saplings, the sound levels that Chris Johnson, a PhD student, has been measuring are, on average, about 45 decibels. That's uncomfortable on the ears. We can also smell it: diesel fumes, in particular. I can even feel it at times; the passing of a massive road train sends waves of vibrations through the ground beneath our feet.

When we emerge from the undergrowth, only a few metres from the edge of the road, the tumult of sensory input is overwhelming. Continuous traffic – including a lot of large trucks – sends the sound meter way up: between 60 and 80 decibels. Anything above 53 dB is regarded as medically damaging. Pulses of fumes and dust clog the air. Auditorily, it's an assault. Visually, it's a kaleidoscope of colours and fragmentary shapes, blurred together in a constantly moving wall of malevolent metal.

I am both horrified and fascinated by roads. They are an essential part of modern life, and the main component of a terrestrial transport network that connects people and cities all over the planet. They allow people, goods and commerce to move unhindered. But their impact on the natural world is a global catastrophe. One estimate is that 10 million animals die from vehicle strike every year in Australia alone. Roadkill is horrendous and upsetting because it is so visible. Far more significant, however, is the effect roads have on the places where these animals live. As the worldwide transportation network expands, it fragments the landscape, isolating many species, especially smaller, ground-dwelling ones, in increasingly severed – and separate – populations.

With colleagues from around the world, a diverse coalition of concerned people has been trying to find ways to lessen the effects on wildlife and biodiversity. This emerging and important field is known as road ecology. One of its main goals is to overcome the barrier effect of linear transport infrastructure, thus enabling animals to move safely through the landscape. Another aim is to minimise the impact on people: injuries, death and vehicle damage form the other side of the coin. This vital and fascinating work has resulted in studies and collaborations with like-minded colleagues from Malaysia to Sweden, Canada to Singapore, over the last couple of decades. It all started in the early 2000s, right here on Compton Road, in the southern suburbs of Brisbane.

There's a quirky routine I perform whenever I'm assessing a new (to me) road, anywhere in the world. I stand a few metres back from the tarmac and the moving vehicles and try to imagine I'm a local animal that needs to get to the other side. I've been a badger in Holland, a clouded leopard in Borneo and an ocelot in Texas. Here in coastal Australia, a typical denizen of this type of subtropical forest might be a northern brown bandicoot. These ground-dwelling, nocturnal marsupials – who always seem to be on the verge of a nervous breakdown – have poor eyesight but supersensitive noses, capable of sniffing out grubs and worms deep in the soil. If *I* can hear, feel and smell the traffic, they must surely be overwhelmed. Nonetheless, they still attempt to cross the many lanes of traffic, with predictable and tragic results.

Every year in late summer, young males leave their homes to make their fortune elsewhere. Sooner or later, they will encounter a road. That is inevitable. Roads are everywhere. If they are lucky, it might be a quiet country road with little traffic. If not, it might be a death trap like Compton Road, with virtually continuous traffic 24/7. We have evidence that some species have learned – the hard way – to cross roads in the small hours, when there are fewer vehicles. Not bandicoots, however. They are most likely to be travelling just after dusk, coinciding with peak hour. The chances of making it across a road at that time are virtually nil.

Bandicoots, in addition to having no road sense, seem oblivious to the deluge of nasty and unpleasant emissions caused by all those machines passing by. Other species have the opposite sensibility and typically retreat as far as possible from any form of human disturbance. That works if the patch of habitat they live in is big enough. But one of the insidious realities is that the ever-expanding road network is continually fragmenting and dividing the landscape, often leaving wildlife stranded in islands isolated by roads.

But being able to move freely is essential for many species as they search for food and mates, avoid predators and rivals, or – as with the bandicoots – disperse away from their natal area. Being confronted by roads severely limits these options. Any species stuck in a fragment of habitat will have an increased risk of competition and inbreeding, and fewer reproduction opportunities. Isolated populations are also much more vulnerable to being wiped out by a catastrophe such as wildfire, storm or serious disease. Animals need to move despite the presence of roads. But how can they make it safely to the other side?

I MET MARY O'HARE – SENIOR PROJECT MANAGER responsible for transportation infrastructure for Brisbane City Council – when we were part of a reference group formed to come up with ideas about how to get wildlife safely across Compton Road.

This was an entirely new challenge for everyone. The group included members of local environment and community organisations, many of whom were seasoned activists and used to the obfuscation of bureaucrats. When Mary walked into our first meeting, we expected the typical 'us and them' confrontation. It didn't go quite as planned.

Mary looked around the room, introduced her staff briefly and then listened attentively as each of us expressed our concerns about the proposed new road upgrade. When she spoke, she was confident, but not defensive as we had anticipated.

'Listen,' she said with an unexpected openness. 'Let's do this differently. It doesn't have to be a fight. Your forest is magnificent and precious, no question; I walk through it almost every weekend. We have to protect it and the animals that live there as much as possible.'

To say we were stunned would have been an understatement.

'So, let's make a deal,' Mary continued. 'We have to build this road – that's a given – but let's make it the safest f...ing road in the country! I'm good at building things, but this project is something completely new to me. I have no idea what needs to be done for the wildlife. That's your job: come up with sensible, practical ideas, and I'll listen. I'm willing to consider just about anything. We have to get this right!'

As we were still registering these surprising words, she concluded: 'I love a challenge. I hope you do too. I want this to be a project that is noticed all over the country, and maybe around the world!'

About five years later, Mary and I stood at the top of a small hill, surrounded by a typical subtropical open eucalypt forest. Around us were slender grey gums, a few angophoras and plenty of wattles, although some looked as though they might have reached the natural end of their lives. A dense and scrappy shrub layer extended down the gently undulating slopes of the hill, merging with the forest on either side. The ground was covered in a mixture of open grassy spaces and leaf litter, exuberant tufts of wallaby and blady grass, as well as a few local weeds. In other words, it looked exactly like a subtropical eucalypt forest, typical of any remnant of natural bushland in coastal Queensland. Mary looked around at this somewhat boring bit of bush with a huge grin. And then unexpectedly, enveloped me in a huge bear hug. 'We f...ing well did it!' she says, with undisguised satisfaction.

What was remarkable about this unremarkable scene was that this forest on a small hill was completely artificial: every kilogram of soil and every single plant (except a few weeds) had been placed here, directly or indirectly, by human hands. It rested on the new hourglass-shaped overpass, which was 70 metres long, 15 metres wide at the mid-point, and 20 metres wide at the splayed ends, and allowed this enormous mound of soil and vegetation to span the four lanes of the endlessly busy Compton Road.

A series of carefully spaced telephone poles with a pair of horizontal wooden beams near the top marched over the hill. They were not for electricity. These were glider poles, theoretically providing a way for local gliders – sugar, squirrel, greater and the rarely seen feathertail glider live in these forests – to cross the road without needing to descend to the ground.

As well as the overpass and the glider poles, there were two other ways for animals to cross safely. Above the traffic, three canopy bridges, made from heavy-duty marine rope, connected the forests on either side of the road with a flexible climbing platform for possums and other arboreal species. Beneath the road, two large, specially designed underpasses, furnished with ledges and a raised wooden beam, had been built during the construction of the road itself. The wooden beam, which sat on metre-high poles, spanned the entire length of the underpass, providing a hopefully safe way for animals to make the crossing without needing to move along the floor.

In all, these provide a variety of ways for animals to cross the road safely. Of course, a crucial feature is the extensive lines of exclusion fences that completely prevent access to the road. Any animal moving towards the road will meet one of these specially designed fences. As they turn and move along the fence, looking for a way through, they will be led to one or other of the crossing structures.

On the very first day after construction stopped, Mary and I were invited to inspect the Compton Road Fauna Array, to use its formal name. We were impressed by how our sketches on paper and many suggestions had been turned into reality. To this day, Compton Road has the largest and most diverse series of crossing options ever constructed in Australia in one location. Of course, this was all theoretical; we had no idea whether any animals would actually use them. Mary was her forthright self: 'After all the effort and money,' she said with a steely look, 'they had better work!' There was little I could say until we finished monitoring. I just grinned sheepishly and crossed my fingers.

Such scepticism was shared by plenty of people. When Brisbane City Council announced that it was building a lot of weird and wonderful structures so that wildlife could cross roads safely, some in the media called the project an appalling waste of money. 'Struggling rate payers to pay for Cane Toads Highway!' bellowed one newspaper. 'Build it and I'll bet they won't come!' declared a popular television personality. If I'm honest, I was also concerned. Experience from overseas suggested that it can take a long time before the local wildlife are game to go anywhere near what had been an extremely noisy construction site over an extended period. It might be months, if not years, before the first creatures dared explore what was, after all, something completely new to them.

We waited impatiently for six months before starting to monitor the crossings for evidence of use. This delay gave the local animals plenty of time to become accustomed to the structures. Monitoring was a crucial step: it was no good simply building these things. We needed solid evidence that they were being used, by which species, and how much. This involved a range of techniques, including installing motion-activated cameras on the canopy bridges, the overpass, and at the entrance to the underpasses. Inside the underpasses a wide layer of fine sand was laboriously shovelled onto the floor and carefully smoothed so that footprints of the animals passing through could be identified. On the glider poles, special 'hair tubes', which had sticky pads on the inside, were set up. These collected a little fur of any unsuspecting mammal passing by. Regular searches for droppings were also undertaken over the surface of the overpass.

At the start of the monitoring, I explained to our small

team that while some animals would use the structures, these would probably be the common local species, and that we shouldn't expect too much. 'I think more animals will use the big open overpass rather than the underpasses,' I speculated. 'This is an extension of the bush on either side, so animals won't really be aware that it is an artificial structure. But the underpasses are completely different. They're cold grey concrete tunnels almost 90 metres long. It's about as unnatural as it's possible to be.' Finally, being realistic, I warned them not to expect much action at the beginning of the monitoring. 'It's only been six months since this was a noisy, dusty abomination. It could be a long time before anything dares come close.'

I was delightfully wrong on every one of these predictions.

The first shock was how quickly animals began to use the structures. At the time, the entire region was in the grip of a prolonged drought. To keep the plantings alive, a complicated trickle irrigation system was set up. A network of plastic piping directed life-saving water to each plant. This seeped down into the thick layer of mulch that had been spread over the entire surface of the overpass. The mulch contained a variety of grass seeds which responded quickly and vigorously to being watered. Within a few weeks, the entire artificial hill had turned bright green as the grasses germinated and grew rapidly. With most of the region parched and dusty, this massive mound of succulent greenery was an obvious magnet for every grass-eating animal within miles. The landscapers arriving just before dawn each day found red-necked wallabies, swamp wallabies, eastern grey kangaroos and brown hares grazing on the verdant sward. 'Thankfully they were after the grass and not the tube-stock,' one of the workers told me with a relieved grin.

By the time we started monitoring the overpass some months later, much-needed rain had reduced the severity of the drought and the number of grazing animals we detected fell to just a few. Our collection of scats (droppings) and camera trap images added several new species – common brushtail possums, echidnas and, unfortunately but unsurprisingly, red foxes – but all in modest numbers. This was hardly surprising; the overpass was still a mainly bare exposed hill, and the plants were still small. It would be years before anything resembling proper habitat developed, so we were reasonably pleased with these early results. We could, at the very least, claim that a decent variety of, as expected, the larger mammal species were using the overpass. It seemed like a good start.

If we were happy with those initial results from the overpass, we were shocked at what emerged from monitoring the two underpasses. If I had done my 'imagine yourself as a local animal' routine – say as a tiny marsupial carnivore such as a dunnart – peering into a cold, dark concrete tunnel would hardly have been inviting. And it was long, especially if you were only a small animal. It's hard to imagine any small creature walking into that. And yet again, my intuitions proved completely misguided.

Dunnarts, along with antechinus, echidnas, native and introduced rodents, bandicoots, possums and a large variety of skinks and snakes showed little hesitation in heading through the underpasses. What was most spectacular was the steady increase in numbers as the weather became warmer, with the peak occurring in late summer. That first January session yielded an astonishing forty-two individuals *per night* using the underpasses! A significant proportion of these late-summer sojourners were young male northern brown bandicoots, dispersing as their instincts dictated, but this time they could venture out safely.

By the time we wrapped up the first intensive monitoring session, it had been a year since the end of construction. Most of the hundreds of tube stock planted all over the overpass were thriving, but were not even a metre high. The overpass was still a strange, stark, mainly bare hill straddling a noisy motorway. It would take time to develop into proper habitat. But already we had recorded a powerful response to the sceptics (ourselves included) who had asked, sardonically, 'Yeah, but do they work?' We could now say with a straight face: 'Yes, they do; spectacularly!'

And that was without hyperbole; none of us had expected this level of animal traffic, certainly not within the first year. It was as though the animals had been waiting impatiently to get across to the other side. They couldn't simply wander onto the road now, of course; the exclusion fences were doing their job very effectively. And like the wallabies using the overpass well before they were supposed to, we suspected that plenty of species were using the crossing structure as soon as it was possible to get though or over them.

What about the structures provided for the arboreal species? Unfortunately, the fancy – and expensive – cameras installed at the ends of the canopy bridges didn't work. The low-tech hair funnels, however, showed that squirrel gliders, sugar gliders, common brushtail possums and common ringtail possums had all left strands of fur behind.

Those sticky pads also showed that both smaller glider species had climbed onto the glider poles, although the much larger greater glider had not. It was two full years before we had solid evidence that gliders were actually gliding between the poles. This was because Brendan Taylor from Southern Cross University decided to force the issue. He captured several squirrel gliders, attached tiny radio transmitters to their backs and released them on the *other side of the road!* Two – presumably furious – gliders returned to their home areas via the glider poles within an hour. Brendan concluded that this would only have happened so quickly if those animals were already familiar with the poles.

The glider poles, canopy bridges and underpasses were all available for use as soon as they had been installed and many species appeared to get used to them relatively quickly. The overpass, on the other hand, underwent continual change as the planted vegetation developed and grew. In the relatively humid and warm subtropical climate (and after the drought had broken), the plants grew rapidly. In 2011, about six years after the completion of the structure, we undertook a detailed comparison of the vegetation community on the overpass with that of the natural forest on either side of Compton Road. Over this fairly short period, the artificial planted habitat already resembled the surrounding forest. The only significant difference was the height of the trees; that was hardly surprising, given the saplings had only been in the ground for six years.

It was about this time, when the plantings had developed into a proper habitat and provided a continuous if narrow corridor of vegetation from one side of the road to the other, that I had two major revelations. It was almost embarrassing to admit it, but both had been staring me in the face for years.

The first concerned birds. You'll be aware that most birds can fly. However, some birds will not fly over an open area devoid of cover. These are mainly the small, forest-dwelling songbirds, that remain concealed within the understorey, venturing out of the cover to forage nervously before disappearing back into the thicket. I knew this, but hadn't thought about how it related to roads.

I was watching a small group of red-backed fairy-wrens flitting about in the thick shrubs close to the exclusion fence. Suddenly, the male – resplendent in his military scarlet and coal-black uniform – appeared halfway up the mesh of the fence, peering out toward the road. For a moment, I assumed he was about to lead his family across the road. But it was over 90 metres to the forest on the far side. Fairy-wrens struggle to fly between bushes only a few metres apart; there was no way these tiny birds were ever going to travel that distance. And it wasn't simply how far they would need to fly; it was how exposed they would be en route: a quick snack for a sparrowhawk or harrier passing by. The problem wasn't the endless procession of trucks and cars passing by – it was the size of the gap between the forest edges.

That should have been obvious. But I had fallen for the simplistic 'birds can fly' axiom and hadn't even considered what roads meant for a large number of small forest birds like robins, finches, scrubwrens and others. Other small species have no problems flying across open spaces. Some, such as yellow-faced honeyeaters, silvereyes and warblers, undertake massive migrations, clearly undaunted by the road network. For birds such as fairy-wrens, however, a two-lane road might as well have been a solid brick wall; they were never going to cross. This means that even modest roads represent an impassable barrier for birds like these. Populations severed by a road are permanently separated. They may be able to hear prospective mates calling on the other side, but will never be able to meet them.

Unless, miraculously, a vegetated overpass is constructed, providing cover all the way to the other side. When the plants growing on the Compton Road overpass eventually became continuous understorey, for the first time in decades – many generations, in bird lives – the populations could be reunited. This was a very significant and unexpected benefit of what I had originally thought of as a mammal passageway.

It was Stuart Pell who took on the task of investigating which birds used the overpass to cross Compton Road. Stuart had been a nutritional scientist with a passion for birds and an astounding work ethic. When he retired, he finally had time to take bird research seriously. He was immediately drawn to the many barely scratched questions surrounding birds and roads. Working on the Compton Road overpass was an ideal opportunity for someone as dedicated as Stuart.

The first project Stuart undertook was finding out which birds and how many were crossing the road via the vegetation on the overpass. Most field studies of birds are conducted in the early morning, when they are most active. While acknowledging that this was unequivocally true, Stuart said: 'But what are we missing during the rest of the day?' I had little to say in response.

To investigate this issue, Stuart set up a chair and small desk within the understorey, with a thermos of tea and a basket prepared by his wife containing sandwiches and biscuits. With notebook and pencil in hand, he began to observe, very carefully, all the birds that passed by. He was there all day (that's nine hours). For sixteen days! 'That's what was necessary,' Stuart told me, matter-of-factly. 'It's the only way we can be sure.' I wasn't going to argue. He also recorded the birds which crossed the road away from the overpass, as a way to find out which ones didn't need the structure and which ones did.

Stuart's findings were detailed, reliable and illumin-ating. While most species were indeed active and con-spicuous during the first few hours of the day, these birds were engaged in finding food. After this critical refuelling activity had been completed, however, travelling became possible. Stuart recorded steady numbers of birds passing through. These species were 'on the move'; they were on the overpass because they wanted to get to the other side. They weren't there to forage, remaining in the dense foliage on the overpass as they crossed. These included three species of fairy-wrens, whistlers and the eastern yellow robin, all forest-dwelling insectivores. Other small species (silvereyes, pardalotes and fantails, for example), however, flew undeterred across the road above the traffic.

This brings me to my other major revelation. Like those birds which used the overpass primarily to get from A to B, I had simplistically assumed that the structure was a conduit enabling animals to cross safely. After all, they are described as 'crossing structures'. Even as I described the developing vegetation growing on the overpass as 'habitat' and remarked how like the natural forest on either side it was, I still didn't twig. With every passing day, this large, contrived hill looked less artefact and more accurate replica. So convincing, in fact, that some animals might see it as somewhere to live.

It was the herps that made me see what I had been missing. And it was Mel McGregor who pointed out, pointedly, that there was more to vertebrate biodiversity than birds and mammals. Mel is a herpetophile, someone fanatical about reptiles and amphibians (collectively known as herptiles, or just 'herps'). Of course, I knew that, but I was still hopelessly biased towards fur and feathers. Mel added scales and cold skin to the mix. She joined the Compton Road team, with her main project being to compare the diversity of reptiles and amphibians on either side of the road, and to confirm whether any were using the overpass.

Detecting these secretive animals required a new technique: pitfall trapping. Pitfall traps are simply buckets buried in the ground so that the top is flush with the surface. A short fence of firm plastic mesh is placed so that it runs over the middle of each bucket. When an animal encounters the fence, it will turn and walk along it, and hopefully fall into the bucket. They remain there until very early the following morning, when the research team quickly releases them.

Mel's study revealed that the local forest had a remarkably rich diversity of herpetofauna, with twenty-nine species being detected in total. This included five amphibians and a wide range of skinks, legless lizards, geckos and dragons. A number of snakes were also seen during the work, but they were all too fast to be identified; they also seemed to be able to escape from the pitfall buckets.

The big question was: would any of these animals be found on the overpass? It was one thing for some birds to travel though the understorey, or for a bandicoot to wander over the structure to get to the other side. It was an entirely different story when the animals were much smaller and less likely to travel far. These types of animals lived in the leaf litter, under logs and rocks, and hid under tree bark. In many ways, this was the real test of our attempt to construct – from scratch – somewhere that frogs and lizards would feel they could settle down. Would our artificial environment be acceptable to these species?

The answer was, again, a spectacular 'Yes!' Mel found an astonishing nineteen different species on the overpass, almost all of which were living there permanently; they weren't simply passing through. Most were fairly common species, typical of urban landscapes in this region. Still, it was reassuring to find them on the overpass. But what was much more exciting was that five of them (a frog and four skinks) were species normally found only in undisturbed forests. To discover these animals was a powerful vote of confidence in the 'natural' condition of what was actually an entirely artificial habitat. I'd love to say that's what we planned; in reality, it was what we simply hoped!

Mel made another extraordinary discovery that further demonstrated the significance of a well-vegetated overpass. This time it involved bats. There are two types of these flying mammals: the huge, so-called megabats, or flying foxes, which use their eyes and noses to locate flowering trees and ripe fruit; and the little ones, microbats, that hunt for insects in the air using sonar. The high frequency calls produced by microbats are far too high to be detected by human ears, but fancy new technology enables us to turn these vocalisations into visual patterns. Plugging special microphones into a smart phone or iPad reveals the presence of microbats in the night sky above; otherwise, they are entirely invisible and unknown to almost everyone.

Mel wanted to find out which species of microbat lived in the forests on either side of Compton Road and whether the road affected their activities. She also wondered if any bats used the overpass. She recorded a huge number of bat squeaks for almost a whole year. What she found was that the bats really did not like the road, with most of their foraging activities conducted well away from the traffic. That made sense; the traffic produced a plume of fumes that are lethal to insects, which avoided the road as well. What was completely unexpected, however, was that the hottest foraging spot by far was directly above the overpass itself. It seemed that the aerial insects were congregating in and above the trees on the structure, making it a particularly rewarding place to forage. This was a world-first discovery. And more powerful evidence of the value of vegetated overpasses.

At the time of writing (March 2025), Australia had a total of eight fauna overpasses, with a further three in the early planning stages. The Netherlands, a country 0.5 per cent the size of Australia, has sixty-six. However, Australia's first was constructed in 2001; the Dutch – and many other European countries – started well before then. The oldest overpasses in the world were installed in France in the 1950s. Today, fauna crossing structures have been constructed throughout the world. Species as varied as African elephants and Swedish moose, Bengal tigers and Singaporean pangolins, Bornean orangutans and Brazilian howler monkeys, are routinely crossing roads that were once death traps. Road ecology is a rare good news story in the otherwise grim arena of human impacts on the natural world.

# (6)

## CONSERVATION by COMMUNITIES

AMOS LOMUNYAH LOBULU IS WORRIED, ALTHOUGH he tries to hide it. Most of the others haven't noticed, but when he isn't explaining wildebeest migration or pointing out the almost invisible lions resting in the shade of the acacia trees, he drifts away to stare into space. It might look like he's surveying this extraordinary landscape, but I know what he is thinking about: Joyce, his daughter.

In the distance, if I follow the direction of his gaze, I can just make out his village away to the north-east. It's that constellation of tiny flickering points of lights on the horizon. One of them will be the kerosene lamp Faith, Amos's wife, has lit as she prepares tonight's meal. She will be calling for Joyce to bring in the honey from the beehives on the edge of their Maasai village. The hives are a new project, providing another item they can sell. The hives also keep any troublesome elephants from trampling through the village. Joshua, their older son, will be helping the men herd the cattle into the boma, where they will be safe for the night behind the dense, thorny fences.

Although I had been communicating with Amos for years as part of my research on conservancies, this is the first time we have met in person. The Maasai are generally a reserved people, not given to overblown emotional expression, at least not with strangers. Yet when I emerged from the little plane we had arrived in, he embraced me like a long-lost brother. Before either of us said anything, he held my forearms and looked deeply into my eyes. I felt he was assessing whether his internet-based impression of me was anything like the real person.

When he finally spoke, his words were initially surprising: 'Tell me, my friend, how is your daughter?' But, as I learned during our many exchanges, a defining feature of Maasai culture is: family always comes first. In an early Zoom meeting connecting Brisbane and Kenya, we had exchanged the basics of our respective families. When Amos discovered that I had a daughter the same age as his, we immediately bonded over our mutual concerns for their welfare and prospects. Both Joyce and Manon were just completing high school and their futures were far from certain.

The reality, however, was that my daughter lived a privileged life in a wealthy, developed country where the options were many. She had just spent a gap year in London, working as a nanny, before commencing university studies. Although we were proud and impressed by her independence, she was not challenging deeply held cultural traditions and customs. You see, Joyce wanted to be a wildlife guide, like her father. She was fit, smart, determined and remarkably mature for her age. There were two significant obstacles to her plans, however. First and most obvious was, of course: she was a female. And in Maasai culture, girls don't leave home to study at a distant training college, far from their family and land. Girls stayed in their communities, helped their mothers, married, and started a family. For Joyce, these things could wait; she wanted to tell the world about her country's incredible wildlife.

The other problem, much more fundamental, was money. These days, prospective wildlife guides were required to attend the Wildlife Tourism College of Maasai Mara. This can be expensive; prohibitively so for most people. The early years of the Covid pandemic had been catastrophic for tourism everywhere, but especially among the conservancies where the money provided by the tourists goes directly to the community. Without visitors there was no cash flow. Although visitors were now back to pre-pandemic levels, money was still in short supply. Paying for a young person to be trained was simply out of the question. And, as usual, the boys were supported before the girls, a situation that weighed heavily on Amos. Joyce and Amos's predicament was one of the reasons for my visit.

This desperate situation was one of the reasons for my visit. Along with a small group of people who had previously visited this place – the Selenkay Conservancy in southern Kenya – we had established the Maarifa Foundation, a charity providing financial assistance to local families so they could continue their children's education. The Foundation initially paid school fees, and for uniforms. Recently, we had branched out, building a library supplied with books and other teaching resources. Our original plan was to wind down once the community was back on its feet. But the many benefits of the Foundation's involvement – and the overwhelming support of the Selenkay community – had convinced us to keep going.

TODAY, I HAVE JOINED A SMALL GROUP OF OTHER visitors on a tour of the nearby Amboseli National Park. It's the end of an eventful day and we have driven to the top of a prominent lookout called Observation Hill. As we disembark from the vehicles and look around, Amos invites us to behold the view. It is, indeed, breathtaking. In every direction, a vast panorama of flat African savannah spreads out to the horizon. Darker patches of scattered acacia trees are interspersed through the broad grasslands. In the direction of the setting sun, the light sparkles and glistens from a multitude of waterholes, marshes and rivulets. The air is cool and still; the harsh bark of a zebra and the unmistakable roar of a lion drift up from somewhere below. We can't see them now – it is too far, and too dark – but around us are tens of thousands of African animals, preparing for the nightly interplay between predator and prey, the cycle of life and death that keeps this vast ecosystem functioning.

As is the custom, we are enjoying 'sundowners', clinking our G&Ts and toasting a wonderful day. It is only one of many remnants of British legacy found everywhere here, in what used to be called British East Africa. As if to confirm this legacy, an English visitor, Enid Colder 'from

Dorch'ster' (as she has told us numerous times) raises her hand.

'Amos,' she says, 'I'm a little confused about who owns the land around here. You seem to suggest this whole region belongs to the Maasai. So how does Amboseli National Park fit in?'

Amos adjusts the red shuka wrap around his shoulders before replying. No matter the situation – unruly children, an unexpectedly close lion, a misunderstanding with a rhino – he always speaks thoughtfully, his voice deep and authoritative, yet quiet.

'Madam, that is an excellent question,' he says. 'There are some important things, however, I do need to say before I answer your question. You need to know a little of the history.' The quiet gravitas of his voice brings everyone to attention. We all lean closer.

He explains that Maasai people had always lived throughout the interior of East Africa, in what is now northern Kenya, and around the fertile lands surrounding Lake Victoria. The colonial era, as was the experience for local people everywhere, had catastrophic impacts on the lives and livelihoods of these proud cattle herders. The seemingly random imposition of political borders – most critically, the separation of Kenya from Tanganyika (now the mainland part of Tanzania) – disrupted ages-old migration routes used by these famously nomadic people forever.

The most important impact was the establishment of the massive 'game reserves', three of which – Maasai Mara, Tsavo and Amboseli – were on Maasai land (as were Serengeti and Ngorongoro, just over the border in Tanganyika). The 'game' in the title is indicative: the British were certainly conserving the game but, at least initially, so they could hunt the larger species. These places were for wealthy Europeans to kill 'Kenya's magnificent wildlife' on their days off!

'These were always our lands,' Amos has stated many times. The Maasai had moved nomadically through this vast open landscape for many centuries; this was their proven survival strategy. Reading and predicting the rainfall patterns allowed them to follow the best pastures for their cattle. At irregular intervals, a community would pack up their few possessions, folded into layers of cow-hide, and trek to the next grazing locations. It was a stable and ecological lifestyle. But it relied on open horizons, and on ancient travel routes being available.

When the massive game reserves were established (Amboseli was proclaimed in 1948) in southern Kenya, the local Maasai took little notice. They didn't realise how the strange and wasteful habits of the Europeans would impact them. They could shoot what animals they liked; the Maasai would continue to live as they always had. 'Although we could never understand the point of slaughtering animals for no apparent reason,' Amos says. 'They didn't even eat them!' Perhaps surprisingly, the Maasai do not hunt; they are the only African people not to use wildlife as a resource. They rely entirely on their cattle for food, milk and leather.

Unfortunately, it wasn't as simple as ignoring the colonials and carrying on. The reserves were designed to preserve the massive herds of wildlife for tourists. At first at Amboseli, the Maasai were allowed into the reserve, especially the vast Ol Tukai (or Lake Amboseli) swamps. This region lies in the vast rain shadow of Mount Kilimanjaro, the massive mountain to the south of Tanzania that prevents rainfall reaching the area. However, an abundance of underground springs originating beneath the mountain feeds a large area of swamps and wetland. Even in the most severe droughts, this complex system of waterbodies never goes dry. It is one of the main reasons Amboseli has such a rich fauna.

For the Maasai, access to these swamps was essential. During the periodic droughts, they would take their cattle to Ol Tukai and stay as long as was needed. It was a vital refugum. At times, herds of up to 80 000 could be present, along with enormous numbers of wildlife species. For these cattle herders, being able to utilise the wetlands was a fundamental right.

Around the time the game reserves were reclassified as national parks, the attitude of the government-installed managers began to change. The presence of Maasai cattle in a national park, especially in large numbers, was regarded as contrary to the idea of 'wildlife preservation'. In reality, the government's priority was always going to be attracting the largest numbers of paying tourists, giving them (in the words on all the shiny brochures) 'the best wildlife experience on the planet'. After paying good money to see giraffes and elephants, being confronted by a herd of cattle accompanied by their Maasai owners was not the impression of untouched nature the visitors needed to see. Increasingly, the Maasai found their access thwarted and their presence within the park resented. These contrasting ideas of what the land represented had become a fundamental and alarming difference between the official government – as the commercial operators of all Kenya's national parks – and their nomadic neighbours.

THE SUN HAS DIPPED BENEATH THE WESTERN HORI-zon and it's time to pack up and return to our campsite at the Selenkay Conservancy. When we emerge from the vehicles and the engine noise stops, an almost miraculous quiet descends and envelops the camp. It's not silent, though.

We are startled by a strange electronic squabbling sound. It's the go-away-birds – yes, that is their name! These brazen and clever camp followers are always on the lookout for an unguarded plate of food. Sleekly grey and magpie-sized, their permanently raised crest suits their fearless disposition.

I notice that all of us are still standing quietly, enjoying the myriad small noises after the racket of the vehicles. The cooler air is a tapestry of insect buzzes and chirps and ... yes! ... the roar of a lion. Immediately followed by the sinister cackle of a hyena. The African night shift has begun.

We all wander off to our tents to rest and prepare for the evening meal. As soon as I turn towards my accom-modation, a Maasai man materialises from the darkness and silently guides me along the dirt path that joins the dispersed sleeping tents to the central hub of the camp. These nightwatchmen patrol the vicinity, staying out of sight unless needed. Their job is to ensure that none of the larger predators comes too close. There is no real danger even if they did but, as Amos explains, 'It makes the visitors feel safe.'

When the bell chimes, announcing that the evening meal is ready, we all wander towards the light and activity. The staff welcome us, as they do for every meal, with beaming faces and warm handshakes. Waitresses, waiters, cooks and the chef, all come out to shout a greeting. They then return to their roles, taking orders, delivering trays of drinks and pouring wine and beer. At the back of the dining room, there is a large display of Maasai gifts and keepsakes: vividly coloured beaded jewellery, small stone and wood carvings of African animals. Several women, one with a small baby strapped tightly to her back, wait patiently for the diners to finish their meal. The Maasai are famous for the brightly coloured beads threaded into intricate necklaces and bracelets, a tradition the women have maintained for centuries. Being able to sell these sets to the tourists is a win–win: the tourists can't get enough, and the women are happy to sell them. A trio of teenage girls, grinning and giggling, stand behind the woman, supposedly learning the tricks of the trade.

Amos, who always eats his simple traditional meal with the staff in the kitchen, joins us at our table when he is finished. One of the visitors asks him about the girls waiting in the gift shop. Are they locals?

Amos grins. 'Yes, very local,' he says. 'In fact,

everyone you can see lives in Selenkay village, a short walk away. That's why you staying here is so important to us. Everything you spend goes directly back to the community – *this* community. That is the main reason successful conservancies survive and prosper. When the benefits of tourism are clear to see, the community is more than happy to work hard.'

Amos pauses and a wistful expression appears on his face. 'Opening the conservancy has provided many opportunities for all members of our community. I thought my daughter might enjoy working in the gift shop, like some of her friends over there. But she is usually too busy. She has other ideas, much bigger ideas.'

I know enough about the history of Selenkay Conservancy and of the many tensions that still exist to know that Amos carries a heavy burden. As well as being one of the main game guides, he also serves on several decision-making committees that oversee the field operations of the conservancy, the finances, and the running of the local school. Cultural, historical and pragmatic, as well as intensely personal dimensions intersect. Balancing these requires a clear and steady vision, thankfully something he clearly has. His clear thinking and deep cultural commitment have enabled Selenkay to become one of the most successful of Kenya's conservancies. But this has not been easy.

Amos was a young man when his father invited him to attend what would turn out to be a profoundly important meeting. A wealthy businessman had approached Eselenkei Group Ranch, the leaders of the local community with a startling proposition. He wanted to lease a large amount of the community's land and turn it into a wildlife sanctuary. His plan was to bring tourists who would pay to see the wildlife, but in strictly controlled numbers, so that their experience would not be tainted by hordes of other tourists. Crucially, he also wanted the community to take on the wide variety of roles that this venture would require. It was an opportunity for paid employment right here in Selenkay. This concept of community-based conservation – a conservancy – rather than through traditional government-owned national parks, was very new in Kenya. The businessman invited the community leaders to go away and think through all of the implications – and there were many.

Virtually every aspect of this proposal was bewildering. But it was also remarkably timely. Recent years had been tough for these people whose primary concern was looking after their cattle. It had been drier than usual, and the condition of their cattle had declined. They were confronted by lower market prices and increasing numbers required for negotiating a bride price. As Amos had mentioned on many occasions, when a Maasai cannot sleep, 'It's always because of our cows'.

But there was an even more serious concern for the entire Maasai nation: the relentless pressure on their culture to change. It would be fair to claim – certainly Amos did so often – that no tribe anywhere in the whole of the continent were as proud of their unique and colourful culture as these nomadic cattle-herders in East Africa. Facing enormous pressure, and sometimes violence, they have withstood the incessant calls to change, catch up, move on, modernise. While some change is inevitable, the Maasai have managed to retain the essence of their culture: their distinctive dress, ornaments, diet, dance and religious beliefs. These characteristics have made them among the most recognisable African tribes, drawing tourists from all over the world to witness their remarkable dances and purchase their colourful necklaces and hand-dyed fabrics.

Most significantly, the centrality of cattle in every aspect of their lives was the biggest issue of all. Cattle literally define the Maasai. They often told us: 'Cattle are our bank.'

Managing their herds was becoming increasingly difficult, however. The closure of the traditional migration routes had meant the end of their nomadic life. Fences became one of the biggest obstacles. Many were forced to settle down in one location and manage their herds as sedentary rather than nomadic pastoralists. This was something they had never done before. And the life had never been easy, especially when it came to interacting with the modern world. For young people, the attractions and temptations of the big city – in this case, Nairobi – were ever-present. Many families had stories of their kids leaving home to try to make their fortune, some never to return.

The arrival of the conservancy proposal, with its extraordinary offer of paid jobs and the involvement of the entire community, seemed too good to be true. Everyone had heard stories of rich white knights making grandiose offerings to desperate landholders, only for the reality to be very different after all the papers had been signed. The Selenkay leaders were smart. They were also aware of the opportunities that could flow to the community. Over the next few weeks, every evening was occupied with frank and detailed discussions around the campfire. Everyone who wanted to speak was listened to. While the benefits of becoming a conservancy were numerous, the risks and downsides were very real.

'The first dilemma we faced was the wildlife,' Amos explained. 'Selenkay simply didn't have the diversity and numbers like Amboseli. The main reason was that the land had been used for many years as an intensive cattle-grazing place. As wildlife habitat, it was no good, heavily overgrazed. Wildlife is important to us, but not our main concern. We didn't hunt or interfere with animals – except when a lion takes a liking to our cattle. They are very easy prey, nothing like hunting a zebra or gazelle.'

If they were going to become a viable conservancy, there was no way of avoiding something truly difficult with powerful symbolic meaning: to allow the land to regenerate properly, they would have to remove the cattle. Not completely, of course. This was a proud Maasai community. Cows were always going to be central to their way of life. But this strange new arrangement required changing their focus to wildlife. The cattle were moved to another part of their land, allowing the habitat to recover after decades of grazing.

In the end, the community came to a unanimous decision: they would lease the land to the company and begin the process of becoming Selenkay Conservancy. This was a momentous event. It would also soon become a major trend, involving hundreds of other communities throughout Kenya, and beyond. Community-based conservation of Kenya's spectacular wildlife (rather than in overcrowded government-owned national parks) had begun.

This new way of living didn't begin instantly. Progress was slow, sometimes contentious, often tedious. The numerous positions and jobs necessary to run a tourist facility in the middle of the African bush had to be filled, and people trained appropriately. They would need people with skills in hospitality, administration, office management, finances and bookkeeping, cooking and kitchen duties, sales and promotion, as well as wildlife guiding. The infrastructure had to be designed, purchased or constructed: roads, buildings, waste disposal, lighting, power generators, field vehicles.

While all of this was going on, something extraordinary was happening out in the savannah. Thankfully, the rains that season had been plentiful and sustained. In the absence of herds of cattle, the ground cover responded quickly: first, a vibrant green sward, then a dense knee-high sea of swaying succulent grasses. This bonanza of fresh foliage began to attract the grazers: impala, waterbuck, Grant's and Thompson's gazelle, Grevy's zebra, African buffalo, and the extremely rare gerenuk. This is an elegant and slender antelope with a remarkably long neck. They often stand on their hind legs to reach foliage well out of reach for other browsers. Naturally, the predators soon followed: cheetah, lion, leopard and African civet. The civet is cat-sized but not a feline. Despite its gorgeous bold black and ginger markings, it is almost impossible to see as it hunts for lizards and fruit in the tall grass. Imperceptibly, mysteriously, tentatively, other less conspicuous species gradually ventured into the land: mongoose, savannah hare, dik-dik and duiker. These are all moderately sized grazing species, and the favourite food of many predators. It's no wonder they are all shy and remain hidden in the undergrowth. The dik-dik is terrier-sized, while the duiker is the smallest of all antelope.

Skip forward a couple of decades and Selenkay has one of the most diverse communities of large mammals and birds in East Africa. It has one of the largest populations of African elephant on the continent – with the largest tusks! And the highest density of birds in Kenya. Amos is still incredulous at how quickly it all happened: 'All we did was move the cows out!'

Amos is, understandably, immensely proud of the achievements of his community. Having been present at every step, he has seen how much progress has been made and the benefits that have come to his people. He is also most aware of the importance of education. 'Knowledge is the key to our survival. Educating our children is our most critical challenge. But it is worth it. The success of Selenkay Conservancy has meant our people have security and certainty.' Over the years, several young people have moved away temporarily to be trained in hospitality or office management, but most have returned, though not always to their original community.

Amos himself served an apprenticeship at the Ol Kinyei

Conservancy after graduating, near the famous Maasai Mara National Reserve, before returning to Selenkay. When asked why he went to the Mara, he mentions the wildebeest. I'm sure that the fact that a young woman named Faith who he met at the training college came from another Amboseli Maasai community had absolutely nothing to do with it!

A FEW DAYS LATER, WE ARRIVE BACK AT SELENKAY Camp. The contrast with our experiences in Amboseli National Park could not have been more stark. Most striking had been the number of vehicles encountered while we were in the national park, all bulging with tourists. At one point we saw seven vans surrounding a cheetah and her cubs, some parked only metres away. Amos couldn't hide his disgust: 'All those drivers know they're not allowed to leave the road, but look at this!' Although we saw a remarkable number of species as we travelled through Amboseli – some in huge numbers – at times it felt more like a theme park than a wilderness.

On our tour through the conservancy, there were only two vehicles carrying six people. Even at the busiest times of the tourist season, only twenty visitors are allowed to stay at any one time. During our visit, we were the only people in the entire conservancy, and our local drivers knew every part of the place intimately. It was, of course, their land and they were proud to share it with us.

We drove very slowly with everyone keeping a close eye out, but we never managed to see anything before

Amos. While the Amboseli had a greater quantity of game, it was the diversity of species we saw in the conservancy that was breathtaking. This included extremely rare and shy antelope such as gerenuk and kudu, as well as all the familiar gazelles, warthogs, buffalo, leopards and lions. If I'm honest, I was especially excited to see so many birds that were new to me. These included an enormous secretary bird, who strode confidently past in search of its favourite food: snakes. This huge creature is unique: a powerful bird of prey which hunts by running rather than flying. Its sudden appearance caused a momentary panic among the vast flock of helmeted guineafowl who were wandering about somewhat absent-mindedly. How guineafowl survive in such profusion when there are so many predators nearby is a genuine mystery.

There was a lot to recall and discuss when we settled down for dinner that night: did anyone identify that gigantic bird of prey? What was that tiny antelope?

Amos joined us as the meal was ending and the other visitors began to leave. We had important business to attend to, the main reason for my trip to Selenkay. I was here to represent the Maarifa Foundation. The director of the foundation, Kristy Thomson, would be speaking to us shortly via a video link, about a new initiative. While the technology was being set up, Amos gestured to a woman and teenager who were waiting for customers at the gift shop. They were obviously nervous about approaching strangers, but we made them feel welcome. 'My blessed wife and wonderful daughter,' Amos said proudly, unable to hide an enormous grin. So here were Faith and Joyce.

'It is so good to meet you,' I said. 'We've heard all about you from Amos. He's very proud of you, Joyce.'

'You are the man from Australia and Maarifa?' asked Faith. 'The bursary we received from your foundation meant Joyce could complete her schooling, during the terrible Covid years.'

Joyce stepped forward and stood directly in front of me, as though preparing to give a little speech. She was barely seventeen and as tall as I was. In a calm, confident voice, she said, 'I and my family are very grateful for your assistance. I learned very many things about our land and its animals. Now I want to tell others. But it is very expensive to go to the training school. I'm not sure what I can do. Do you have any suggestions?'

At that moment, the technician called us over to the laptop, now showing the beaming face of Kristy. We all gathered around as Amos introduced his family and the staff who were present. After a bit of housekeeping and discussion about the next round of high school bursaries, it was time for the main item on the agenda.

'We are particularly excited about the Maarifa Foundation's new initiative,' said Kristy. 'We've been supporting the schooling of your community's children for a number of years. Now it's time to make a much bigger step. This new phase represents our long-term commitment to Selenkay and to the future of conservation in Kenya through the conservancy movement. Tonight, we are proud to announce the first training scholarship for a worthy student to attend the Wildlife Tourism College of

Maasai Mara. The recipient will become a fully qualified wildlife guide.

'There is something very special about this very first scholarship,' said Kristy. 'The most promising student is a female. I am so excited to announce the first recipient is … Joyce Namunyak!'

We hadn't planned for Joyce and her mother to be present, but it was just as well they were.

The family stood in shocked silence as the news sank in, their mouths open in astonishment. Suddenly, they ran together and embraced, Joyce somewhere in the middle.

THE MAARIFA FOUNDATION, WHICH STARTED IN 2017, continues its close connection with the Selenkay community, as well as several other Maasai schools in the region. The Maarifa Wildlife Guide Scholarship is offered every two years. The 2025 recipient is Anthony Lapiyia Lenkishon, who, I am happy to say, is a keen birdwatcher (but that had nothing to do with him being selected – the criteria are strictly adhered to).

# (7)
## FARMING for GOOD

I GREW UP ON A FARM. THERE WAS ALWAYS TOO MUCH sun, too little rain, wild dogs and foxes, kangaroos in the lucerne, crows killing lambs, weevils in the wheat … I would listen to Mum and Dad talking in hushed tones after I had gone to bed. In hindsight, I can see that they were struggling with elemental forces daily: drought, hail, erosion, flash floods, corrupt agents, Labor governments and city-bred greenies. A backdrop of brutal natural forces with an endless caste of villains set the stage for what seemed like a relentless, exhausting battle.

Therefore, there was a palpable sense of relief when we moved into town after my father landed a job at the local farmers co-op. A regular wage after the uncertainty of the annual wheat and wool cheques – which were usually inadequate – was like a gift from heaven.

Yet there was also the inescapable impression that we had given in, taken the easy way out; caved, unable to take the pressure. A cushy job in town came with a distinct loss of face. This was reflected in romantic notions of 'life on the land', talk of 'being fulfilled by honest toil', even the unselfconscious mention of 'belonging to the country', a remark apparently made without irony.

There's a new appreciation for the way Indigenous peoples lived with the land – or, as they put it, on Country. Landscape-level management by the original peoples over vast periods of time gradually transformed the entire continent, allowing the sustainable use of natural resources for millennia.

In contrast, the settlers applied farming approaches imported from western Europe in utterly different conditions. Those approaches have led to many places being rendered useless and unproductive. Many will never recover. The thin topsoil has long since blown away, the inevitable consequence of overgrazing, compaction by millions of hard hooves and erosion following the removal of all the protective vegetation. On a continent of thin, infertile soils, the loss of the meagre topsoil effectively means the land is dead. The vagaries of the Australian climate, especially inland, have often resulted in heartbreak: droughts that lasted decades; rain so heavy it washed away entire crops and herds of livestock.

It dosen't have to be like that; there are other ways to work the land.

WHEN LOUISE AND DAVID MOVED TO THEIR UN-assuming farm in the foothills of the Snowy Mountains, they had little in the way of experience and even less of an understanding of how to use their land. Refugees from the Big Smoke of Sydney, they were leaving behind stress, heartache, and workplace trauma. And they were naïve to the point of ridiculousness, as they freely admit. Their only experience of the 'bush' was as avid bushwalkers and birdwatchers. They weren't even convinced that they could or should farm their bit of land. They had never drenched a sheep, mended a fence, or dug out a bogged four-wheel drive.

Their original motivation for purchasing the property called Highfield was primarily its conservation: the property contained a significant amount of Box Gum Grassy Woodland, an extremely endangered ecosystem in eastern Australia. Highfield adjoined the large Ellerslie Nature Reserve, meaning that 'their' woodland was part of an extensive continuous habitat and not an isolated patch. Managing Highfield carefully was a rare opportunity to contribute something meaningful to conserving a vital and important ecosystem.

Conservation is all very well, but they also needed to make a living.

'It took us a while to accept the inevitable,' explained Louise. 'At first we didn't think much beyond trying to conserve the woodland. But we needed some kind of cashflow. And given that this place had been a farm – well, that was a fairly big hint.'

Although a proportion of the place would be set aside entirely for conservation, most of it was typical pasture that for decades had supported lots of sheep and cattle. There were also shearing and farm equipment sheds, fences, dams and all the usual noxious weeds you get in this part of the world.

'We were adamant that we didn't want to farm in the European way,' said Louise. 'We had no idea how, but we knew there had to be a better way to use the land as a business. It didn't have to be a war against nature.'

One thing in their favour was that they were acutely aware of how much they didn't know. Admitting they needed to learn and were likely to make mistakes was to become key to their survival. They were willing to watch and learn.

The first big decision was to buy a mob of sheep: a special breed called Dorpers, robust, chunky-looking animals that don't need shearing. It's not wool they provide, but meat: excellent lamb, a highly sought-after product in many high-end restaurants. When the first group arrived and were running about exploring their new home, Louise and David felt elated and a little sick. Could this possibly work?

I had stumbled upon Louise and David's place when looking for somewhere to hide away and write for a while. A friend had found a delightful looking 'eco-hut' called Kestrel Nest that could be hired, not far from Adelong and the Snowy Mountains, on a property called Highfield. It seemed ideal as a writer's retreat. From the blurb on their website, this couple seemed to have a rather different philosophy on how to run a farm.

'Would they mind telling me more about their approach?' I asked in an email. To say that Louise's response was positive would have been an understatement.

'Come and see for yourself!'

AS I DRIVE UP TO THE MODEST FARMHOUSE, I'M wondering what to expect. I've been emailing Louise, and had recently spoken on the phone with her, but I can't picture the people or the place. Sure, I've seen some gorgeous shots of enormous guard dogs and adorable little black-faced Dorper lambs, but images online can be more art than reality.

Before their dramatic treechange, Louise and David had lived in Shanghai, Cambridge and trendy inner Sydney, working as academics and senior administrators. And now: farmers? That's a lot of upheaval and readjustment. And I knew that the decade since they had arrived at Highfield had included the slow-motion trauma of drought and the near-death experience of a colossal wildfire that came close to ending it all.

The dull thud of my car door closing brings a couple of enormous off-white dogs (for a moment, I am reminded of polar bears) bounding up to greet me with barely contained enthusiasm.

'Hey, be polite!' And there she is, Louise, looking as though she has just helped birth a calf while uprooting scotch thistles with her spare hand. It's been ten years since she moved from their fashionable Federation terrace in Sydney. The person striding towards me and beaming broadly looks like she has made the transition to life in the bush with her resolve strengthened and sense of humour enhanced.

After a brief introduction, Louise explains that the other half of this partnership, David, is driving to Wodonga to deliver soap made from lamb suet and then on to Mullegandra to pick up a bull. 'That's the sort of thing we have to do these days,' she says with a shrug. Then, without wasting a moment, she rubs her hands together and says: 'So let's go! The best way to understand what we're doing is to see it up close.' She signals for me to jump into a battered four-wheel drive and we are off at speed.

Louise talks excitedly as we career along the dirt road, pointing out places of interest and remarking on a dozen topics, all somehow related to their attempts at sustainable farming. She says that we are heading to a significant location, a place that exemplifies the particular challenges she and David have faced since they purchased the property. The vehicle slides to a sudden stop, enveloping us in dust. We clamber out into the sparkling sunshine of a magnificent clear June day, the sky an impossibly rich blue.

'Welcome to Sheep Camp Hill,' Louise announces with a grand gesture, her arms outstretched. 'This was one of the most disgusting places on the whole property. Boy, did it stink!' We walk further up the slope and stop near a weedy patch growing on what looked like thick, black dirt. 'This isn't soil,' Louise explains, bludgeoning the ground with the heel of her boot. 'It's compressed sheep dung. Generations of sheep camped on this hilltop. It was a safe spot, giving a good view in almost every direction. You get dingoes, foxes and wild dogs here, but at least the sheep could see them coming.

'Concentrating lots of sheep in one spot for ages means an incredible amount of sheep shit. You could smell it from a kilometre away! And when it rained, a noxious black sludge flowed down the slope to the creek. Almost no vegetation would grow where the sludge went, and that led to serious erosion after heavy rain.'

Clearly, something needed to be done, Louise explained. This single location was having a detrimental impact on a significant area of land.

The first thing they did was straightforward: fence the area so that the sheep could no longer camp there. There were shady trees down the slope they could use instead. That part was easy, relatively speaking. The new fence encircled the site and effectively joined it to the adjacent conservation area.

Much more difficult was how to rehabilitate the now sheep-free site. It was a bare, rocky, sun-baked patch, devoid of even a blade of grass due to the soil compaction by millions of hard hooves and reclining sheep bodies. And toxic levels of nitrogen from all the sheep dung meant few plants could survive.

'We started by planting lots of native seedlings,' Louise said, 'and almost none survived. That wasn't surprising – it's a tough and toxic place. But it was disappointing to spend so much time and energy digging and planting for so little reward.'

This experience, however, gave rise to a fundamental revelation. Sometimes it's best to leave things alone and let nature do the work.

'We drove past Sheep Camp Hill every day, so we were able to monitor what was going on,' Louise said. While most of the seedlings they planted died quickly, an entire ecosystem of weeds began to develop spontaneously. Within a few weeks, a mini-forest of Paterson's curse, milk thistle and capeweed appeared.

'Those plants had to be bloody tough to survive those conditions. You have to admire those so-called weeds for that.'

The attitude of Louise and David's neighbours was not so positive. The forest of bright green noxious weeds growing on the rise was conspicuous from far away. It was unsubtly pointed out that something needed to be done. Which meant, obviously, kill the lot with herbicide. Now, if not sooner. Growing up in Wagga, I witnessed this almost instinctive response among farmers: remove weeds immediately, in any way possible. Failure to do so was an indication of laziness, stupidity, or both.

'But what about curiosity?' said Louise. 'By then, we were starting to develop a different perspective. What would happen if we just let those weeds grow? Let nature do her thing? It wasn't a popular decision. And one more reason for the locals to suspect we were just a little crazy!'

This 'do-nothing' approach wasn't out of sloth or bloody-minded contrariness. Louise had learned at university about a process known as ecological succession, the way that the plants in a community gradually change over time. The classic textbook examples were from newly formed islands. These gradually become vegetated as seeds are blown in or arrive with bird visitors. To begin with, there are only a few hardy mosses and grasses, but eventually shrubs and bushes follow. In time, there might even be a forest. But this process takes a lot of time and plenty of luck. It was the same at Highfield; they had to wait and see (and ignore the muttering neighbours).

During the first year of 'do-nothing' on Sheep Camp Hill, the Paterson's curse and thistles grew tall and luxuriant while the capeweed formed a thick groundcover. Over the years that followed (the neighbours had by now given up in disgust), the size of the thistles diminished. At the surface, something mysterious was happening: a rich bed of decaying organic matter began to form. With the normal cycles of rain, frost and the occasional hailstorm, the base of decomposing plant material from dead weeds developed into a humus layer, transforming the oversupply of toxic nitrogen into the foundations of a proper soil profile. This was the foundation for a succession of annual weeds.

Eventually – it took about eight years – the dominant community on the hill become a mix of perennial native grasses. The weeds? Gone completely! (Apart from the one spot that Louise had shown me.) This outcome had been their hope all along. And the best part? It happened by doing nothing. This experience became one of Louise and David's leading philosophies: 'Sometimes it's best to leave well alone.'

'People seem to think that to get what you want from the land, you have to use brute force, spend lots of time and money, do something big and, well – masculine,' says Louise. 'The traditional approach to weeds is to poison everything in sight, or rip the ground up with a manly bulldozer. We've found that a different approach works even better: a gentle nudge rather than a massive shove.'

In the case of Sheep Camp Hill, the nudge was simply to fence the sheep out, and leave the rest to Mother Nature.

'*Now* look at it!' Louise says, turning to face the site, her arms spread out in welcome. 'It's been a long time, but there isn't a weed in sight. It's all native grasses. The weeds did their important job early in the succession process and then became part of the humus layer, and that let the native grasses thrive.'

She takes in the sight with obvious satisfaction. 'You know what this patch would look like if we'd done the normal thing and blasted the place with poison? Exactly the same as at the beginning! Weeds galore. Sickening stench. Toxic run-off. Case dismissed!'

From the site of this unexpected triumph, we wander down the slope about 100 metres and stop to take in the extensive view. The horizon to the south is the continuous mottled green of a healthy grassy woodland. Somewhere among the trees is the boundary between Highfield and the adjoining nature reserve. There's a fence hidden behind all the trees, but only humans would notice. The scarlet robins, dusky woodswallows and turquoise parrots couldn't care less. They move about freely within this extensive wooded world that stretches continuously back to the hills behind.

Those small birds, however, rarely leave the cover of the shrub layer growing inside the woodland. To venture out onto the open pasture below would be too dangerous, making them easy prey for one of the spotted harriers or collared sparrowhawks we have seen out on patrol. There are similar species living in the large remnant patch of woodland where we are standing, explains Louise: we can see fairy-wrens and finches flitting about in the shade. But the birds living in these two areas would never normally meet: the wide-open spaces between these woodland patches might as well be in another galaxy. There was simply no way that most of the smaller bush birds would ever traverse that vast open area without cover.

Louise points to the broad expanse of pasture between the wooded areas. 'See those big trees down there? Most are ancient. They're remnants of the original woodland that once grew all over this landscape. Although they're spaced wide apart, and isolated, they're vital as stepping-stones, allowing all sorts of animals to move across what for many is a dangerous and exposed landscape. Lots of larger birds, but also gliders and even reptiles, will sprint from tree to tree until they're safely across the plain. But for most of the smaller, shrub-layer birds, like fairy-wrens, robins, finches and scrubwrens, even those trees are too far apart.'

Unless the distance between patches of safe cover was shorter; then they might try. And that is exactly what Louise and David are organising.

'If you look along that ridge you can see where we've planted new trees – twenty-five, to be exact. Yellow box, red box and Blakely's red gums all local species, in the spaces between the old trees, hopefully making the journey more possible for those birds. Oh, look … there! Yellow-faced honeyeaters! They've just flown from the closest tree, that enormous Blakely's over there. Right on cue, to prove my point!' She claps her hands in spontaneous appreciation.

'Of course, a few new trees do not a woodland make. Over the whole property we've added over three hundred so far, and that will continue. We're also planting lots of dense shrubs in the spaces between the trees. These will give the tiny birds what they need most: secure hiding places. The plan is to eventually have a thickly vegetated corridor about 30 metres wide connecting the treed areas. It's slow going, but we're in this for the long haul. When we're gone, we want to feel that we left this little bit of Earth in better shape than when we found it.'

I point down to the valley below, toward conspicuous lime-coloured vegetation growing in the lower part of the valley, becoming quite extensive in the flatter areas.

'Ah, yes,' says Louise, with the now familiar lilt to her voice that precedes a particular interesting story. 'That bright green stuff is a mixture of reeds and *Carex*, a native sedge that grows brilliantly in wet patches. You can see how it follows the creek line. What it does is capture rainwater runoff – it filters the water and slows down the flow, which flood-proofs the valley and protects the farm dam further down the slope. Without it, the dam would be full of silt and sheep dung in no time. Those reed beds are also another seriously endangered ecosystem.'

The zone is also vital habitat for all sorts of animals such as quail, native rats and mice, while their predators, mainly black-shouldered kites, nankeen kestrels and harriers, are often lurking nearby. Louise also explained it is valuable as a refuge for young lambs when the winter winds blow. In other words, it's one of their most important ecosystems. Unfortunately, not everyone sees *Carex* in the same way.

'Soon after we moved here, we met an enthusiastic young agronomist, just out of uni,' says Louise, with a wry smile. 'He'd heard us raving about our whacky plans and philosophies. He generously agreed to come out and give us some advice and asked us for a written brief to guide his suggestions. Great, we thought; free expert advice. We spent a long time on the brief, explaining our philosophy and motivations as well as emphasising that we were raising sheep for their meat.

'He came out a week later. After a tour of the place, we ended up exactly where we're standing now, the spot with the best view of the main paddock and surroundings. "I've got a pretty good idea of how you can maximise your productivity," he said. "What you need are 550 superfine wool Merinos and make that your mainstay."

'We listened with growing alarm.

'"First thing, though," he said, "that reed and sedge area down there? Useless for sheep. Inedible. I'd nuke it asap. A couple of rounds of Roundup followed by burning should do the trick. Then seed the whole area with *Phalaris*, an excellent grass you can import from South Africa. You'll be making good money from the wool in a few seasons."

'Our young agronomist friend apparently didn't notice the looks on our faces or the insincerity in our voices as we waved him goodbye. But he was hardly out of earshot when my normally cautious and polite husband exploded. "He didn't listen to a thing we told him! Except 'sheep'. I know we're new to this game, but what on earth was he thinking? And he actually said 'Nuke the sedges'! That's an endangered ecosystem!"'

Louise paused and turned around to face me. She looked thoughtful. 'As I reflected on his "advice",' she said, 'I realised: we really are not following the traditional way of farming.'

And that has taken both courage and resolve. Over the years, Louise explained, some farmers have changed their approach after seeing what was possible on Highfield. Others think they're bonkers. 'It was just one more reason for people to regard us as odd. But it also made us even more determined to do things differently.'

It was time to move on. Afternoon tea beckoned and with a secretive grin, Louise said, 'Let's show you the Nest.'

We clambered back into the vehicle and drove steadily up a rough dirt track, a precipitous drop on one side. We went through a few gates, and after carefully navigating a traffic jam of black-headed sheep who insisted on walking on the road directly in front of us we turned a corner and headed steeply downhill.

And there it was, the Kestrel Nest. The cottage stood as a solitary sentry point, more light and space than metal and wood, overlooking a vast landscape of forested hills, a clear winding river and expanses of native pasture. The cottage and a water tank were the only human-made structure visible in the entire landscape. It would be hard to picture a better place for solitude and thinking. I knew I'd be coming back.

With steaming mugs of tea and slabs of homemade fruit cake, we sat on the spacious veranda, enjoying the quiet and the view down to the Yaven Yaven Creek. Louise, with some hesitancy, explained the origin of the name Kestrel Nest. A solitary kestrel was the only living thing they saw in the area for two weeks following the catastrophic fires in 2019–20.

'The cottage was only half-built at the time, and the flames came within a few metres of completely destroying everything. The only reason it's still here is because of the extraordinary efforts of several fire crews – from the National Parks Service and the local Rural Fire Service – who worked around the clock to save it.' Louise paused for a moment; the memories of that traumatic time were obviously still vivid. 'We'll never forget the support we received from the community during that time. That was when we realised what real care and support means out here.'

The experience of living through those fires, when literally everything they had worked so hard for looked like being lost in an instant – including their lives – had led to a new perspective on life. Like many others directly affected by those fires, they could have concluded that living out here was too risky. They could have fled back to the city and a far more predictable life.

But that was not seriously considered. The reality of the multiple crises facing the planet is impossible to ignore. Rather than pack up and retreat, Louise and David felt even more strongly that their activities on a small bush property were one way they could make a difference. Only at a very local level, obviously. But it was also keeping hope alive. And that itself was something worthwhile.

# (8)
# FEEDING a NEED

AT THE VERY END OF RESERVATION ROAD ON THE outskirts of Taintor, Iowa, are two large electronic display boards. You might have seen these outside schools and churches, displaying news, forthcoming events and witty quips. But these two have been set up facing each other, in the front yards of the last two houses. The content of these two billboards is somewhat unusual. For example:

| | |
|---|---|
| 23 HOUSE FINCHES BETWEEN 6.30 AND 7.00 AM. BEAT THAT! | EASY! 5 CARDINALS AT THE SAME TIME! |

It doesn't matter that almost no one ever reads these messages. They are meant for an audience of one: the fellow living opposite. For years, it had been a source of friendly, often humorous, banter.

But a few weeks ago, the tone of the messages changed.

| | |
|---|---|
| KEEP YOUR DISEASED FINCHES AWAY FROM ME | WINTER IS COMING. DON'T YOU CARE? |
| WE DON'T NEED MORE CHICKADEES. WE NEED MORE WARBLERS. | FED BIRDS SURVIVE THE COLD. GOOD LUCK! |

This was one of the reasons I'd paid a visit. These two friends had very different opinions about bird feeding and as I was in the States speaking about this subject, I wanted to find out why.

Reservation Road starts as a typical suburban street, lined with typical bungalows with typical lawns and rosebushes. By the time it reaches the boundary fence of the Taintor Nature Reserve, however, it's a lot less typical. The last two houses are set back on much larger blocks and surrounded by an atypical amount of vegetation: lots of tall trees with a diversity of dense understorey shrubs. Far more than is typical of a small town in the midwest.

The people most likely to make it to the end of the road are desperate teenagers looking for somewhere to make out late at night. They are unlikely to notice the signs and don't usually stay for long. The owner of the place on the right has rigged up an immensely powerful spotlight aimed directly at the place the cars usually park, seemingly hidden behind a hedge. He waits exactly 6.5 minutes before flicking the switch. What had been a dark, secluded spot is suddenly illuminated by blinding light. As I said, they don't stay for long.

These two houses are the homes of Syd Wilcoxen and Bill Ngato. 'It's a quiet street,' they say; they don't need to add 'and that's how we like it'. Bill and Syd have been friends for the last twenty years, after Bill moved into the street with his wife Norma. Bill is naturally outgoing, and wanted to get to know his new neighbour across the road. Syd didn't seem to be an easy person to engage with, but Bill kept trying.

One Saturday morning the two men were working in their respective front yards, Bill pulling weeds and Syd planting seedlings. Bill decided to try his luck.

'Your peach tree looks like its gonna have a decent yield this year,' said Bill.

'I guess,' said Syd.

Bill persisted. 'I'm heading into town to check out that new plant nursery tomorrow. Wanna come? They have a lot of new native plant seedlings.'

'No, thanks,' said Syd.

Before Bill could answer, a loud, harsh chattering sound made them both look up. The sound was repeated and, as they watched, a large black and red bird flew past with a looping flight and landed at the top of a tall tree in Syd's front yard.

'Well, I'll be darned. A pileated woodpecker!' said Syd, with unexpected exuberance. 'I've never seen one around here. They're usually only found on the other side of the reserve. I wonder what this one's up to.'

That was the longest speech Syd had produced in years. But even more surprising to Bill was the topic.

'I didn't know you were interested in birds,' Bill said.

'Yeah, I've become a bit of a birdwatcher. It's something I can do without having to deal with people.'

'Have you seen any warblers passing through lately?'

'Well, I think I saw a bay-breasted last week. It certainly wasn't a pine. That was pretty special.'

And that was that. From that moment, the two were firm friends, bonding over the latest sightings and arguing about whether the sparrow Bill claimed to have seen was a savannah or just another song sparrow.

These sevety-something men had retired at about the same time. After thirty-five years as a high school teacher, the last seven as a principal, Bill was more than ready. He had coped better than most with the endless curriculum changes, the pressure and stress, but he was ready to call it a day.

If Bill was happier than he had been for years, Syd was the opposite. A successful engineer, he prided himself on his 'can do' attitude; his ability to solve problems and come up with innovative fixes. He saw the world through pragmatic, quantitative, binary lenses. Every 'problem' had a 'solution'; it was simply a matter of clear and objective thinking. Syd assumed that was how life worked.

On the day after his retirement, he started working on his and Norma's plans for the future, starting with a Grand Tour of Europe, followed by a trip to Australia to visit their son. He heard a crash and turned around to see Norma on the kitchen floor.

'She died on the spot, just like that,' Syd told me. 'The ambulance people said it was a massive heart attack. I couldn't believe it. Still can't.'

Just like that, Syd's world collapsed. He worshipped Norma. She was one of the few people who could put up with his rigid attitudes. The main reason he had agreed to retire was so that he could spend more time with her, trying to make up for years of neglect. The trips and adventures they were going to have would be like a second honeymoon.

That had been five years ago. As he recounted the scene for me, it was clear the pain was still intense.

'I didn't get the chance to show her how much I cared. Now I just feel guilty. And empty.' We sipped our coffees in silence. There was not much I could say.

Across the road, Bill and his wife Betty had lived in their place for almost fifty years. They had raised four boys, now dispersed far and wide. Their eldest, James, had moved to the UK, where he worked for an export business. He wasn't shipping cars or televisions. His role was ordering and and distributing huge amounts of birdseed and bird feeders. That hardly sounds revolutionary, but it has caused a lot of trouble at the end of Reservation Road.

You see, Bill feeds the birds that come to his garden.

Syd most certainly does not.

But let's back up a bit. A little science and history might be useful.

Feeding birds in backyards has always happened, especially in countries that have tough winters. A bit of a sandwich, some leftovers and scraps tossed to whatever birds might have been hanging around, looking hungry. The only commercial bird foods available were for caged birds – canaries and budgies, mainly. These consisted of a mix of seeds such as sunflower and millet.

And then someone twigged that these products could be repackaged and marketed as 'wild bird food', an idea that took off spectacularly. Of course, this was only useful for seed-eating species, but these were abundant, especially in the northern hemisphere, and were more than willing to try this new food. The result was a huge industry based on supplying seed but very little else. All of the other species that consume other sorts of food – insects, fish, fruit, berries, worms – miss out. But most people don't seem to care.

Bill's yard is festooned with an elaborate array of weird and wonderful feeders, all designed to provide seed for visiting birds. There are simple platforms and many tube feeders as well as elaborate multi-head devices. And he keeps adding more. James makes sure that his father hears all about the latest designs and ideas, and Bill is only too willing to take the bait. Neither of them would admit it openly, but bird feeding has brought them back together.

For years, James was estranged from his family. Betty said her two men were simply too alike to ever get on. As a teenager, James had clashed with his father over almost everything. He accused his parents of ignoring him in favour of his siblings. When he moved to England for university, everyone was relieved. For years, there was little contact. Bill didn't understand what had happened. For someone who cultivated friendships, it was painful and confusing. He was always looking for some way of re-establishing contact.

The move to another country gave James an opportunity to reassess his relationship with his father.

When Bill announced that he was retiring and would be devoting more time to his garden, James saw an opportunity. His father already had a few handmade bird feeders and enjoyed watching the birds coming to feed. At Bill's retirement party, the largest present was a heavy parcel from the UK. It contained a Perspex tube feeder with six perches and holes for accessing the seed. Bill was delighted; he hadn't realised that his son was even aware of his interest in feeding birds. He spontaneously sent James a text, thanking him and asking how he was. James replied immediately. It was the first time they had corresponded in over five years. From that moment, they have been in regular contact.

I met Bill by chance at the annual Wild Bird Feeding Industry conference in Des Moines a few years ago. James had suggested to his father that he should attend; it was a great way to hear about the latest advice and practices. Bill had never been to any sort of conference before and was wide-eyed with amazement. What he learned about this industry astonished him. He had no idea of the scale of what he thought was just a private hobby. He had assumed it was a quaint old-fashioned occupation, like growing bonsai or having a saltwater aquarium. He was astonished to learn that 5 million Americans provide food for wild birds daily, distributing a total of 450 million kilograms of seed every year. The US bird food industry had an annual turnover of more than $4 billion. He suddenly realised that his son was involved in a gigantic global enterprise.

'Can you believe those numbers?' were Bill's first words to me – a complete stranger – as we queued for lunch after the first session of the conference. 'I had no idea how enormous this industry is!' I agreed; many of the stats being presented were almost impossible to comprehend. For example, one speaker suggested that we imagine a very long train pulling hoppers loaded with birdseed instead of coal. The amount of seed provided to (and eaten by) birds in the United States every year would fill 22 000 carriages!

When he heard my accent, Bill asked about the situation in Australia. 'Is it the same Down Under? Different birds, of course, but is it as popular as it is here?'

I explained that while a lot of Australians do indeed feed birds, the official attitude among most environmental agencies, city councils, conservation groups and bird organisations was one of strong opposition. Bill looked astounded.

'But why?' he asked.

'It's a bit of a mystery,' I said. 'It's relatively recent. Up until the '60s, lots of bird and nature organisations actively encouraged feeding. There were competitions, instructions for building your own feeder, bird food recipes. But in the '80s, something changed. The authorities said feeding birds spread disease, and encouraged vermin and also unwanted species like sparrows and starlings.'

But the main concern was dependency: the fear that feeding birds would result in them forgetting how to find natural foods, potentially leaving them vulnerable to starvation if the supply stopped. To prevent this outcome, the message was: don't feed them in the first place.

The issue of birds becoming reliant on foods provided by people is not confined to Australia. It's a significant worry around the world, especially during severely cold weather, when natural food sources are hard to find. Although many northern hemisphere birds routinely migrate south to avoid winter, plenty do not. These birds have a tough time simply surviving the winter. Some have suggested that seeing the plight of small birds starving in the snow was the origins of the regular bird feeding seen in Europe. People moved by their apparent suffering began to offer kitchen scraps. Such a response seems natural.

Bill and I decided to skip the next session ('Financing your bird feeding franchise') and found a little coffee stand surrounded by garish plastic and aluminium feeders, some unlikely to attract anything but people with too much money. The coffee was dreadful, but Bill wanted to talk. It was about his troubled friend, Syd.

'Syd's a good buddy, but I've been worried about him ever since his wife died. He was always opinionated, but now he's downright rude. We have these electronic noticeboards set up in our front yards, see? We use them for messages, like bragging about seeing something rare or unusual. Which used to be fun, but since he got back from Australia, visiting his son, his messages have been angry, nasty. He's accused me of spreading disease! When you were talking about bird feeding in Australia earlier, I remembered that that's where he'd been, to visit his son in Brisbane. I wonder whether he picked up some of the anti-feeding messages while he was there.'

'There are certainly some fanatical anti-feeders in Australia,' I said. 'The thing is, most of the reasons against it aren't true – or at least they're hugely exaggerated. I've been researching bird feeding for years. If Syd wants to hear the facts about it, I'd love a chance to talk to him about this stuff.'

At which point Bill asked me whether I could come to Taintor, Iowa, and meet Syd. I had a few days up my sleeve, so the trip was easily arranged.

A FEW DAYS LATER I'M DRIVING THROUGH TAINTOR. It's the epitome of a small town in the midwest: it's flat and picturesque, but surrounded by a monotonous ocean of corn. The only area of forest is within the town itself; centuries of dedicated gardening has resulted in a broad area of leafy suburbs. Beyond the town – apart from the large nature reserve to the north – there is little habitat for most birds. Still, the town supports a decent number of species, many whom visit the many well-stocked feeders.

I pull my rental car to the side of the road to check I'm at the right address. That's when I see the two electronic noticeboards: 'Keep Your Diseased Finches Away From Me' on one side of road, and 'Winter Is Coming. Don't You Care?' on the other.

Bill is waiting for me in his front yard. He gestures for me to pull into his drive. He notices me looking at the message boards.

'The way I responded probably didn't help things,' he says.

After I drop off my suitcase on Bill's veranda, we walk across the road and stop at Syd's front gate. We are both a little uneasy about what the reception might be like. Bill has only managed a couple of perfunctory greetings over the past few weeks, not enough to make any conclusions about Syd's demeanour.

And then from behind us comes a booming voice: 'Well, if it isn't the perpetrator of Crimes Against Biodiversity himself! And he has an accomplice with him this time.'

I turn, expecting see an angry face. Instead, the fit-looking mature man who approaches us looks cheerful and welcoming. After a vigorous handshake he ushers us into his sprawling garden. Bill glances at me with a bewildered expression, as if to say, 'I'm as surprised you are!'

'Your yard's remarkable,' I say. 'You've got quite a diverse collection of plants here. What do your "normal" neighbours think about all the vegetation?'

'That's an Aussie accent, isn't it?' Syd says. 'My son lives Down Under these days, in Brisbane. I saw him a few weeks ago.'

It is hard to reconcile this animated man with the gruff, difficult person Bill has described.

'Speaking of Australia,' says Bill, who looks relieved to see his friend sounding so positive, 'you might be interested in having a chat with my friend here about bird feeding. We met at the big bird-feeding conference in Des Moines.'

Syd raises a bushy eyebrow and scans my face with a quizzical expression. 'Well, now, that is interesting,' he says. 'But first let me show you around my garden.'

As we walk slowly around the large yard, Syd explains that he plants only local native species. He points out some components of this renewed landscape: patches of grassy meadow interspersed between the trees; dense thickets of native shrubs; piles of branches and tree trunks; and several small ponds festooned with floating egg masses. Syd notices me noticing the tadpoles.

'Yep. Plenty of frogs. And newts. And dragonflies. You need more than birds to make up an ecosystem.'

'So it looks like you're recreating the original habitat,' I say.

'Well, trying!' Syd says. After a moment, he adds, 'And I think it's worked as restoration for me, as well as the land.'

We settle into some weathered but cosy armchairs on Syd's back deck with a view of his entire backyard. He has strategically arranged his many plantings so that most of the area is visible from the deck. Several lines of sight enable birds to be spotted, even in the most distant corner. A well-used pair of binoculars lies ready for action near Syd's favourite chair.

'So,' I say, 'I see several bird baths, but no feeders.'

Out of the corner of my eye I see Bill wince, anticipating Syd's reaction.

But Syd takes it in his stride. 'Once, that would have been a red flag to a bull, but I'm older and maybe wiser these days,' he says. 'Look, what I'm trying to do is make this patch a haven for as many species as possible, without artificial food sources. I believe that everything you plant, wherever you are, should be local, so it's adapted for the climate, the soil, even the insects of that area. The bird seed mixes people buy are made up of seeds from all over the world – completely different to what the local birds will have evolved with. We have no idea what that might do to them.'

'Surely someone would have noticed if that was a serious problem,' says Bill. 'At the conference we heard a lot about the research that bird seed companies are doing, making sure the nutrition's right.'

'You're both right,' I say. 'We don't know how these fancy seed mixes might affect the birds. But most grain-eating birds are adapted to using whatever's available anyway – they wouldn't survive otherwise. And, like Bill says, the top bird food companies do a lot of research to make sure their products are clean and well balanced. There's so much competition that anyone who gets it wrong wouldn't last long.'

'Okay,' says Syd. 'But that's not how I want to do it. In Australia, I heard a lot about why feeding's a bad idea, mainly because of the spread of diseases, and the fact that birds might get dependent on it.' He turned to Bill. 'What do you say to that?'

It felt like a genuine query, rather than a baited hook.

'The disease thing is why I keep my feeders clean, so that sick birds don't infect other birds. A few years ago some house finches turned up with pussy, weeping eyes – conjunctivitis. They were pretty much blind by the time they arrived at my place. Those poor birds didn't move, even stayed there overnight.'

'I remember that event well,' I say. 'I had a sabbatical at Cornell soon after that outbreak took off, in the late '90s. The Lab of O – of Ornithology – is there, and they started tracking the spread. It was fast, and deadly. By the time it burnt itself out, about 60 per cent of the house finch population was gone. It spread so quickly because infectious birds – just like Bill said – stayed at the feeders, passing on the disease to all the other birds that visited those feeders.'

'There was a lot of publicity about it,' says Syd, 'but no one said people should stop using feeders. They told them to keep the feeders clean, but I don't think many people are as diligent as Bill. I'm surprised there hasn't been another outbreak.'

Syd is enjoying this discussion, seeming to feel he's scoring points for his side. 'And what about dependency?' he says. 'If there's a permanent food source, why would any bird bother looking for whatever it eats naturally.'

'That happens to be something I've been investigating for quite a while,' I say. 'In one of our studies, we looked at Australian magpies in the suburbs. Half had access to feeders, and the other half didn't. They normally eat worms and grubs they dig up from the ground. This might sound strange, but if you want to attract magpies to your feeder, you don't put out seed, you put out meat. Often it's what we call mince, and you call ground beef, but it's also ham, bacon, salami and dog food.'

'Wait just a second,' says Bill, looking astonished. 'You're saying that people put out *meat* for birds in Australia?'

'Yes, though not for many – just a few insectivores and carnivores. When a breeding pair has access to meat, it's hard to believe they'd bother digging up worms, especially when they've got ravenous nestlings to feed. We thought the fed pairs of magpies would simply stick to the feed, while the unfed birds would keep digging up worms.

'But we were wrong. It turned out that over three-quarters of the food the fed magpies gave their nestlings was natural. If any bird was going to give up looking for natural food and switch to the feeders, it was going to be exhausted parent magpies. But it didn't happen. It was like the magpies had a "no junk food" policy.

'When I looked at similar studies around the world, they all found the same thing: even when feeders are available, most birds still use natural foods rather than relying on the feeders. One explanation is that birds are incredibly good at knowing exactly what they need in their diet: vitamins, minerals, other microelements. They know that the "junk" doesn't have these components, but natural foods do. So they use the feeders for snacks, rather than complete meals.'

The sun is sinking in the west, the temperature is dropping, and the conversation has reached a natural conclusion. Syd stands, says 'I'll be back soon', and disappears mysteriously into the house. Somewhere in Syd's forest, the first birds are starting the evening chorus. Was that a meadowlark?

Syd appears carrying three shot glasses and an ornate glass bottle. 'It's a local bourbon – perfectly legal, of course! For special occasions.'

He pours out three glasses and passes one to each of us.

'First,' he says, 'I'd like to toast my friend Bill, for putting up with his cantankerous old friend.

'Secondly, welcome to our new Aussie "mate", as they say. What you said has set my mind somewhat at rest about feeding. But don't worry – I'm not going to be putting up any feeders!

'And thirdly: to the birds! They've made me a better person. Definitely more observant, and maybe a bit more tolerant.'

And we all raise our glasses to the birds.

# EPILOGUE

ALL NOCTURNAL BIRDS HAVE A CERTAIN MYSTIQUE, a distinctive but hard-to-define presence connected to the fact that they live in the dark. Most fly noiselessly, navigating deftly through the lightless world like ghostly apparitions. Night-dwelling creatures often conjure fear and misunderstandings.

Humans banish the dark whenever they can, fearful of lurking dangers. As a result, large parts of the world never experience true darkness. Night and its fears have been eradicated for the benefit of light-dependent humans. For many of the myriad species whose senses have evolved in the dark, this has been catastrophic. They have had to retreat to the increasingly remote places where artificial light doesn't penetrate. But this is becoming ever more difficult. The almost ubiquitous intrusion of anthropogenic light is just one more way our species has imposed itself on the entire planet, oblivious of its influence on our fellow creatures.

Nightjars are among the strangest of the denizens of the night. It's almost impossible to detect them during the day, even though they typically rest on the ground, often in remarkably open locations. Their camouflage perfectly matches the leaf litter on which they crouch and they only flush when you're about to stand on them. How many times I've simply missed one while searching I'll never know! Their call is as distinctive as it is odd: a deep, loud *glonk glonk* when perched, and a completely different cicada-like trill while in flight.

The large-tailed nightjar has been a particularly sought-after species for me, the limited number of times I've actually seen one adding immeasurably to their allure. For me, they are the epitome of a natural mystery. Their elusiveness and strangeness are undeniable.

American philosopher Thomas Nagel famously asked 'What's it like to be a bat?', concluding that the sensory world they inhabit is so profoundly different to ours that it is impossible to answer his question adequately. Similarly, I've been asking whether we can ever know what's it like to be a nightjar for decades, and have come to much the same conclusion. Everything about their lives is so alien to ours, and so seemingly incompatible with the human world, with its lights, cars and endless other disturbances, that it is remarkable they are still here at all. As each place they once could be found was replaced with cattle, houses or roads, their demise seemed inevitable. Another sad reality of the times; an extraordinary animal petering out in the face of human influence.

And then, for four years, I lived in Kuala Lumpur, the large and sprawling capital of Malaysia. More by good fortune than careful planning, Kuala Lumpur's urban land-scape retains a number of large tracts of tropical rainforest. Having remnants of the original vegetation within a city is one of the most important features necessary for maintaining a rich biodiversity. Despite what may seem self-evident, many cities around the world are species-rich compared to other places. This relates to the reasons these places were settled in the first place. To establish a community that will grow and prosper, the location needs to be fertile, with an abundance of resources. Kuala Lumpur is no different. Today these reserves continue to support an astonishing array of species, including tapirs, pangolins, and hundreds of bird species, including the occasional hornbill.

Only a few weeks after arriving, I was walking along an ordinary suburban road near my home one evening when I heard a most unexpected bird call: it sounded exactly like a large-tailed nightjar! Really? I had been surprised at how many Australian species lived in my admittedly leafy suburb – Brahminy kite, olive-backed sunbird, little egret, spotted dove, white-bellied sea-eagle – but the nightjar? The environment was typical suburbia, though with plenty of street trees and expansive parks, but very few private gardens. We did live close to one of the big rainforest reserves but – as I eventually discovered – the nightjars didn't bother with that. They lived happily and successfully in suburbia. Almost every street had a pair. They jostled for airspace and hawked for moths under the streetlights. Astonishingly, at least some appeared to rest during the day on the flat rooftops. I have no idea where they placed their nests – possibly in some of the numerous open grassy private areas beside government buildings, or amid the undergrowth besides the watercourses.

I present this story as an unusual cautionary tale, and a plea for humility. We still know so little, despite centuries of study. The interactions that exist in any ecosystem are so interconnected in time and space that we currently have no way of understanding how it all works. Nature is beyond our capacity to understand, and is far more resilient than we are. We are undeniably and inextricably a part of it, but we are just one species among unimaginable complexity. Our rise to global dominance is likely to be temporary unless we learn to take our respectful place among the creatures we share this planet with.

# SOURCES, RESOURCES
# and REFERENCES

**PREFACE**

abandonedberlin.com/flugplatz-johannisthal/

Meffert, O.J., Marzluff, J.M. & Dziock, F. 2012. Unintentional habitats: Value of a city for the wheatear (*Oenanthe oenanthe*). *Landscape and Urban Planning*, 108: 49–56.


**INTRODUCTION**

Callinan, R. 2022. Report raises doubt about cause of the bushfire that razed Binna Burra Lodge. *ABC News*, 4 February 2022.

Crutzen, P.J. & Schwägerl, C. 2011. Living in the Anthropocene: Towards a new global ethos. *Yale Environment* 360.

Hines, H.B., Laidlaw, M.J., Buch, W., Olyott, L., Levy, S., Melzer, R., & Meiklejohn, A. 2020. *Post-fire Assessment Report – Natural Values: 2019 bushfire, Lamington National Park, South East Queensland Region.* Department of Environment and Science, Queensland Government, Brisbane.

Twan Eng, T. 2012. *The Garden of Evening Mists.* Myrmidon Books, Newcastle upon Tyne, p. 196.


**(1) WHEN BIRDS BECAME COOL**

Doremus, J., Li, L. & Jones, D.N. 2023. Covid-related surge in global wild bird feeding: Implications for biodiversity and human-nature interactions. *PLOS ONE 18*(8): e0287116.

birda.org/merlin-bird-id-a-comprehensive-app-review/

ebird.org/species/asikoe3

**(2)   TIMING IS EVERYTHING**

Holder, K. & Montgomerie, R. 1993. Context and consequences of comb displays by male rock ptarmigan. *Animal Behaviour* 45(3): 457–70.

Holder, K. & Montgomerie, R. 1993. Rock ptarmigan. *The Birds of North America: Life Histories for the 21st Century*, no. 51.

Montgomerie, R., Lyon, B. & Holder, K. 2001. Dirty ptarmigan: Behavioral modification of conspicuous male plumage. *Behavioral Ecology* 12(4): 429–38.

www.environmentandsociety.org/exhibitions/wilderness-babel


**(3)   WHEN THE HUNTER DIDN'T**

Caldecott, J. 1991. Eruptions and migrations of bearded pig populations. *Bongo* 18: 233–43.

Canon, J. 2023. Bearded pigs a 'cultural keystone species' for Borneo's indigenous groups: Study. *Mongabay*, 20 March 2023.

Cronon, W. 1995. *Rethinking the Human Place in Nature*. WW Norton & Co., New York.

Hazebroek, H.P., Adlin, T.Z., & Sinun, W. 2004. *Maliau Basin: Sabah's Lost World*. Natural History Publications, Kota Kinabulu.

Kurz, D.J., Saikim, F.H., Justine, V.T., Bloem, J., Libassi, M., Luskin, M.S., Withey, L.S., Goossens, B., Brashares, J.S., & Potts, M.D. 2020. Transformation and endurance of Indigenous hunting: Kadazandusun-Murut bearded pig hunting practices amidst oil palm expansion and urbanisation in Sabah, Malaysia. *People & Nature* 3(5): 1078–92.

Love, K., Kurz, D.J., Vaughan, I.P., Ke, A., Evans, L.J., & Goossens, B. 2016. Bearded pig (*Sus barbatus*) utilisation of a fragmented forest-oil palm landscape in Sabah, Malaysian Borneo. *Wildlife Research* 44(8): 603–12.

Miwil, O. 2024. African swine fever threatens bearded pig species in Borneo; may be driven to extinction. *New Straights Times,* 19 January 2024.

Weston, P. 2024. 'The pigs have disappeared': Swine fever threatens food source for millions as disease hits wild herds. *Guardian*, 19 January 2024.


**(4)   ELEPHANT MEMORIES**

Flower, E.K. 2012. Elephants in tourism venues: Exploring elephant welfare and interactions with tourists in Thailand. PhD thesis, Griffith University, Brisbane.

Flower, E.K., Burns, G.L., & Jones, D.N. 2021. How tourist preference and satisfaction can contribute to improved welfare standards at elephant tourism venues in Thailand. *Animals* 11(4), 1094.

**(5)  CROSSING THE ROAD**

Johnson, C.D., Evans, D. & Jones, D.N. 2017. Birds and roads: Reduced transit for smaller species over roads within an urban environment. *Frontiers in Ecology & Evolution* 5: 38.

McGregor, M., Matthews K. & Jones, D.N. 2017. Vegetated fauna overpass disguises road presence and facilitates permeability for forest microbats in Brisbane, Australia. *Frontiers in Ecology & Evolution* 5: 153.

McGregor, M., Wilson, S., & Jones, D.N. 2015. Vegetated fauna overpass enhances habitat connectivity for forest-dwelling herpetofauna. *Global Ecology and Conservation* 4: 221–31.

Pell S., & Jones, D.N. 2015. Are wildlife overpasses of conservation value for birds? A study in Australian subtropical forest, with wider implications. *Biological Conservation* 184: 300–309.

**(6)  CONSERVATION BY COMMUNITIES**

Kenya Wildlife Conservancies Association: kwcakenya.com/

The Maarifa Foundation: themaarifafoundation.org/

**(7)  FARMING FOR GOOD**

www.highfieldfarmwoodland.com/kestrel-nest-ecohut/

**(8)  FEEDING A NEED**

Jones, D.N. 2018. *The Birds at My Table: Why We Feed Wild Birds and Why It Matters.* NewSouth Publishing, Sydney.

Jones, D.N. 2019. *Feeding the Birds at Your Table: A Guide for Australia.* NewSouth Publishing, Sydney.

**EPILOGUE**

Nagel, T. 1974. What is it like to be a bat? *Philosophical Review* 83(4): 435–50.

# ACKNOWLEDGEMENTS

It's hard to avoid all the usual clichés when acknowledging the people who made this thing possible. But it's true: without the attention and care of some critical friends who were willing to read, cringe, cajole and not-so-gently correct early drafts, this would have been very different. If it works, it's largely down to these extraordinarily generous people.

Immense thanks to:

Mark Cocker – one of the best nature writers on the planet. It is a profound honour to count you as a friend and companion at this treacherous moment in history. I urge you to read everything this bloke has written. Please! It's extremely important.

The people who feature in these stories – Karen Holder, Alex White, Emily Flower, Chris Johnson, Stuart Pell, Mel McGregor, Kristy Thomson, Louise Freckelton and David Bray. Your willingness to overlook a little poetic licence in service to a better story is greatly appreciated. I'm utterly indebted to the many suggestions you made and the corrections you pointed out, saving me from eternal embarrassment and no small amount of cultural clumsiness. In particular, Alex's willingness to share her 'love story' and Kristy's gentle guide to Maasai naming protocols are gratefully acknowledged.

Robyn Horwell read every version of every part of this book, made innumerable suggestions and posed critical questions at key points in the book's evolution. Many thanks.

Sincere thanks to Dr Esther Onyango for reviewing the chapter on the community conservation movement in Kenya.

I need to make special mention of Louise and David, operators of the exquisite Kestrel Nest EcoHut, where significant components of this book were written. If you are after a place to write, be inspired or just disconnect for a while, there can hardly be a better retreat. Check it out: www.highfieldfarmwoodland.com/kestrel-nest-ecohut/

I also need to openly express my gratitude to my publisher Elspeth Menzies and editor Emma Hutchinson, whose support has been unwavering throughout our numerous projects together. NewSouth Publishing continue to impress and astonish me with their remarkable combination of professional expertise and personal attention. They make it all look so simple.

I am eternally indebted to the extraordinary skills of my copyeditor, Tricia Dearborn, who tweaked and nudged ever so gently and improved this book in myriad ways. A rare combination of consummate professional, vigilant tense-fixer and tough-love counsellor: thanks so much, Tricia.

I would also like to thank Madeleine Kane for the wonderful cover, which is an instant talking point for everyone I show it to.

My ever-enthusiastic agent, Margaret Gee, has been tireless in looking after the contracts, contacts and collaborations that are an inescapable part of the publishing world. Thank goodness you know how it all works, Marg!

Finally, sincere thanks to my long-suffering partner Liz, who has had to put up with a lot from her endlessly preoccupied House Husband. She even laughed at some of my jokes.

* 9 7 8 1 7 6 1 1 7 0 3 8 6 *